THE CATCHING OF A KILLER

La job de "Ti-Luc Landry"

Josh Ouellette

◆ FriesenPress

Suite 300 - 990 Fort St
Victoria, BC, V8V 3K2
Canada

www.friesenpress.com

ISBN
978-1-4602-9142-9 (Hardcover)
978-1-4602-9143-6 (Paperback)
978-1-4602-9144-3 (eBook)

1. TRUE CRIME

Distributed to the trade by The Ingram Book Company

CONTENTS

In Memoriam

This book honors SSgt Neal Jessop, a great police officer with the Windsor Police Service who served his community and his country with valour, honor and dignity.

RIP Neal Jessop
(Sergeant Major)

My first novel is dedicated to my beautiful wife and our beautiful children who stood by me and supported me over my career in law enforcement. Thank you.

INTRODUCTION

On September 1, 1997, Ronald Lougheed's body was discovered in a wooded area in Windsor, Ontario. He had been shot with a single .22 caliber bullet to the head. The police had few leads on the person, or persons, responsible for the murder. They started putting things together when a local salvage yard operator informed them that someone had sold him a 1979 White Buick Riviera registered to a man named Ken Legace of Windsor. The police seized the vehicle after they found traces of blood on it and in it and further forensic and blood tests revealed that the blood found in Legace's car matched that of Ronald Lougheed.

Legace was arrested. During a series of interviews, he said he knew nothing of the homicide. However, he told police that Wayne Joseph Ross, an aboriginal Canadian with the nickname "Wahoo," had borrowed his car that weekend. According to

Legace, Ross had confided to him at his apartment that he had used the car to dump Lougheed's body. Legace also told police that Wahoo was a friend of his, but Legace was worried that the police would blame him for the crime and "take him down for it," so he gave Wahoo up.

After providing a video statement explaining his non-involvement in the killing, Legace negotiated with police, and an agreement was reached where Legace would get a $5,000 reward, a forgiveness of his more than $700 in unpaid fines, a recommendation for leniency in an upcoming drug-related trial, and expense money if he would assist police with their investigation. The deal also included introducing an undercover police officer to his group of friends, which included William Murdoch Mackenzie, Wayne (Wahoo) Ross, Michael Rainone, and several other individuals who frequented Mackenzie's rental house at 921 Wellington Avenue in Windsor and might have knowledge of or be involved in the crime.

In October 1997, following the receipt of Legace's information, police executed a search warrant at McKenzie's house, and it revealed blood matching that of Ronald Lougheed and a shell casing consistent with .22 caliber ammunition. After analysis, they concluded that, with the traces of blood and the spent bullet found in McKenzie's house, it was the location where Ronald Lougheed had been shot and probably died.

Following the discovery of the evidence, the owner of the unit, William Murdoch McKenzie, was taken into custody and interviewed about his knowledge of the crime. He denied any involvement in the incident. It should be noted that the police believed that Wayne (Wahoo) Ross had killed Lougheed, because that was what he had told Legace.

As expected, William (Billy) McKenzie continued to deny knowledge of or involvement in the homicide, so the police were obliged to release him for lack of evidence. They were convinced that Lougheed had been killed at Billy's house and that Wahoo had borrowed Legace's car to dump the body, but they could not identify all of the people involved or those who were aware of who took the single shot that killed Lougheed.

In the meantime, Wahoo and Michael Rainone were charged with obstruction of justice and related charges for their involvement with moving and dumping the body. Investigators believed that Wahoo was responsible for the homicide, but they needed more evidence, and possibly an admission, so he would be found guilty in the courts.

That's where I entered the picture.

1
THE PHONE CALL AND THE INVITATION

It was a cold day in Bathurst, New Brunswick, and I was busy doing the routine work of a community liaison officer for the local northern New Brunswick police force. That part of my life was probably the most fulfilling and interesting. I got to visit local schools, talk to kids and teachers, visit local service clubs, and anything else that had to do with public relations for the department. I had been assigned the position because of the need for me to be available on short notice to assist in major investigations and undercover jobs. By having me assigned there, it was easy to take a few weeks or months off to disappear somewhere in Canada to do what I loved best—take down bad guys, drug traffickers, and murderers. I was also the liaison person for the Canadian Intelligence Service of Ontario (CISO) in New Brunswick for municipal and regional police undercover operators. On short notice, I could contact an undercover operator (UC) trained by CISO in New Brunswick to be seconded on a job anywhere in Canada. I had done several jobs for the RCMP in my home province, but none like the journey on which I was about to embark.

CISO maintained a pool of officers with specific qualities, credentials, and qualifications. In other words, they didn't send a UC to a biker bar if he or she was a geek, just like they didn't send a straight-acting guy into a gay bar if he couldn't fit in and be comfortable. Each officer had special qualities and training, and CISO, at the request of any police service in Canada, would provide the best candidate for the job at hand.

I was the first graduate from outside of Ontario, and I was followed by many other officers—municipal police officers, because the RCMP did not allow municipal police officers to take such specialty training. Three weeks of intensive undercover police techniques, exercises, and exams were administered by some of Canada's best police officers, and I made it! It was the most strenuous and demanding training I had ever undertaken, but it was also the best. I had found my niche. I was good at it, and I was a natural actor—what some would call a good bullshitter. There was no more satisfying moment in my police career than when my instructors informed me that I had completed the course and, in their words, was qualified to be a UC, a handler, or a project manager (a nice title for the case manager of a specific file).

Undercover operations were another tool that police used to gather evidence, intelligence, and confessions by targeted individuals in a particular offence. The operations were expensive, and they took their toll on the UCs both emotionally and physically. Sometimes they failed to gather the proper evidence for many reasons—bad intelligence, mouthy handlers, arrogant handlers, drunk operators, brown-nosing, budget-conscious police managers, and so on. But there was no better way to convince a jury that some flat face was guilty of a serious crime than when a police officer gave testimony obtained by way of an undercover operation.

Since graduating from training, I have completed eighty-nine undercover operations, mostly on drug cases, prostitution rings, illegal gambling in Toronto, and a few of what the boys called a "cell job." That was when I was sent into a holding cell with an individual who had just been arrested for murder, and the investigators required as much evidence as possible to ensure the case was solid when it went to court six months later. They were looking for details, such as the location of the weapon and a motive.

On one occasion, I was sent in on a cell job with a young man in his twenties who had just stabbed his local bootlegger and drug peddler to death for reasons yet unknown. By law, I was not to question him on anything. I was to let him start the conversation, agree with him, offer support, and so on. So, there I went—long, greasy hair, old clothes, and no dentures—and tried to act like an asshole.

The suspect was brought into the holding cell, where I pretended to be asleep. After a few jittery moments, I opened my eyes, looked at him, and saw a look in his green eyes like he really needed a friend.

Well, Lord thunderin' Jesus, boys, I'm your man, I thought.

He asked me why I was there.

"The cops got me with a key of coke, man," I replied. "Someone snitched on me, and I'm not too happy."

"I'm in deep shit," my new friend said. "I killed a guy last night."

Strike one. He had just admitted to a cop that he had killed someone.

"Tabernacle, what you gonna do?"

"Well, they've been interrogating me for about four hours, and they got nothing on me, except that I was the last one seen entering his house with my girlfriend to buy some dope. They don't have the knife. I threw it into the woodstove of the old house, and it's burned to hell now."

Strike two.

"We were sitting there, my girlfriend and I, drinking beer and cracking, and the old bastard tried to put the make on her. I was pretty stoned and drunk and took offence to that, so, I got up, grabbed a knife, and cut him. It was pretty weird to see the blood gushing from his neck. Afterwards, he gurgled a few seconds, and then he went quiet. It was pretty surreal, man, but he should not have been putting the make on my woman. She's sixteen, and he's fifty-nine. Kind of gross. That old bastard deserved to die."

After some more useless chitchat, my handler came in to rescue me from the psycho. "Get up, Landry, you're on your way to court."

I looked at my new friend, who had fallen silent, and wished him luck. Then he said some pretty heavy words that have stuck with me ever since.

"Yeah, I took the old bugger's life, but he also took mine, didn't he?"

I thought that was pretty deep shit for an illiterate guy who was about to spend the next twenty years in her majesty's jail.

When I left the cell, I told my handlers what he had said to me about the knife, wrote my notes, and left the building, back to my regular job as a community liaison officer. Later, I learned that the blade of the murder weapon was found in the old woodstove and that the admissions the culprit had made to me in the cell was enough to convince his legal aid lawyer that his client should plead guilty and throw himself on the mercy of the court. He did exactly that, and we concluded another successful homicide investigation, sending the psychopath on his way to the slammer.

Small town cops in Canada conduct various duties during their career, from patrol, to drug enforcement, to major crime investigations. Some work as patrol officers for thirty years while others specialize in drug enforcement, major crime investigations, such as homicides and sexual assaults, and some end up in the twilight zone of management. At the beginning of their law enforcement career, most of them are like I was. I sought action, excitement, adrenaline, and events that made my heart rate accelerate and my blood boil. When a tad of fear was added to the mix, I found myself alert and alive.

We say we don't like it, but we strive for those fifteen seconds of glory. Not minutes, cops never get minutes of glory. Fifteen seconds is about it. The rest of the time, they're covering their ass and being subjected to the Monday morning quarterbacks who run the job. Those are the "white shirts." They spend a nice weekend at home with the family, enjoy a good drink, clean the yard, and strategize on how they're going to deal with one of the troops who, over the weekend, happened to have arrested some flat face for beating his wife and kids but in the process might have called him a name or put the handcuffs on too tight or forgot to read him his rights, all the while rolling in the dirt trying to control the animal. But that was okay with me. My wife loved me, and my kids believed I was a good guy. Above all else, I was convinced without a doubt that my dog, Scrappy, loved me, so the hell with them all.

Police officers, especially specialist officers, cannot work the eight to four gig. It's boring, and besides, its daytime, and the bosses are around watching. I felt more comfortable with the people of the night—cops, hospital emergency room staff, paramedics, the Tim Horton's girls. I don't think my managers liked me, because I was one of the above, a little rebellious, strong-willed, and mouthy, especially when I knew I was right.

I was never content with the routine, never happy with the Hollywood portrayal of cops. I had seen real misery, pain, hate, and ignorance, and I had seen our uncaring community leaders went on like they were in another world. The Hollywood depiction of police managers was no stereotype. It went on every day. It really was that way, folks, and it still is. "Make sure the press doesn't know why we didn't arrest that guy, or they might ask questions that will embarrass our illustrious politicians or whoever." If you aren't "one of the boys," you go nowhere in the echelon of police power.

During all my years of service, I felt the pulse of my community—the elderly, who were scared, and the young, who were tormented by the ever-increasing pressures of being a kid. Most cops, including me, believed that we were the last line of defense for such people. Lawyers only cared about the almighty dollar. They told the poor sap they could get him off, ensure his defense until trial day, and then advise him to plead guilty to get a lesser sentence. Don't get me wrong. Most, if not all, of those charged were guilty anyway, so their lawyers figured they might as well get a few bucks from the legal aid system before they threw their client to the mercy of the court. "Do not lose faith, my friend, the Law Society will protect you from those big, bad cops." I didn't have much respect for defense lawyers who used the system for their own needs to the detriment of the young people who needed legal help but could not afford a big time lawyer.

Over the years, many good lawyers have convinced judges and juries that their client is innocent because the cops screwed up or because their client suffered from some kind of temporary illness that caused him or her to beat up, shoot, or rape an innocent victim. It was not always that way. On April 17, 1982, the day our government enacted the Charter of Rights and Freedoms, the Criminal Code of Canada began a long re-evaluation of our laws that is still ongoing, and the burden of proof has changed for police and prosecutors alike. Police officers accept and support the 1982 decision, but it can be very frustrating for police and victims who can't seem to get some criminal locked up. It is easy for our legal community, on Monday morning, to second guess every decision or action a cop made in a split second at two in the morning the previous Saturday. No complaints. We serve and protect. Our country has changed for the better, I think, and I know that things are different now than when I was a kid.

I grew up with nine brothers and five sisters in a good, old French Canadian Catholic family. There were no iPods or Nintendo. All we had was hand-me-down skates and Sears catalogs as shin pads, never mind that Jacques Plante of my great Montreal Canadians still did not have the guts to face his bosses and wear a facemask. We were Canadian kids, which meant hockey in winter and baseball in summer. Ball gloves and broken windows were all part of it. There was no way my parents would allow me to sit on the couch and watch TV. Besides, there were only two channels in those days, and my mom was a busy and sometimes cranky woman. She did not need a bunch of rowdy boys around her when she was preparing supper or baking bread.

"You go outside and play right now, or wait 'til your dad gets home," she'd say.

I was neither impressed nor scared by her threats, at least not openly. After all, the old man was only five foot three, and I could outrun him when he got angry. I always believed that a person ran a lot faster scared than angry. I was scared and my dad was angry and, thus, slower.

One thing about dad though: He probably invented the "good mom, bad pop" interrogation method. Mom would say that I had been bad that day, but not that bad, while Dad took no prisoners. Bad or not too bad did not exist in his vocabulary. If he could catch me, I was guaranteed a friendly but swift kick in the rear. Never out of anger, he said. Great for him, but it still hurt like hell—not so much on the ass but on the ego.

That man could intimidate the hell out of anyone—visiting politicians, the parish priest, the English-speaking neighbors—and he always managed to set them straight. He was a whiz at getting politicians to provide a little token of their appreciation if he voted for them, such as a flask of London Dry Gin (an Acadian favorite in those days), a truckload of firewood for our stove, another truckload of coal for the furnace, or, from the priest, a guarantee of immediate entry into heaven. Nowadays, the courts frown on that kind of stuff, but back then, it was commonplace for everyone. After all, people had to survive and feed their kids.

My dad was an honorable man even if, at the time, I didn't think he was very intelligent. As a rebellious teenage son, I didn't always respect or understand his advice and wisdom, but then a funny thing happened. The older I got, the smarter my dad seemed to get, and now I only wish my kids could understand what I understand now.

Dad's family was poor. He did a little better, but his salary as a foreman in the Dalhousie paper mill in 1967 was only $7,000. From that, he had to make a living, ensure his kids ate and got clothes, and so on. According to the neighbors, we were well off. We even had a two-channel television, and the milkman delivered seven bottles of milk a day at twenty-five cents a pop, which got pretty expensive. My mom would bake several loaves of bread every Saturday, and the old man worked overtime just to make ends meet. Then he would come home and have to deal with the likes of my brothers and me, who had made his wife a little more insane that day.

I think often of my parents, now deceased. How in hell did they do it? I will always honor them. I promised myself at an early age to make them proud someday. My dad would be able to sit with the other old boys on a bench near the old water reservoir and boast about his son's achievements. Even if he didn't get to see me on my biggest case, he was proud enough to have a cop in the family.

"I'm gonna be a police officer, Dad." I told him one day.

"No, you're not," he replied. "I hate those Mounties. They used to chase us when we were kids trying to smuggle booze to the Americans and bring back smokes to Canada"

"I'm not going to be a Mountie," I explained. "I won't get accepted. Your other sons have criminal records, and the federal police won't accept someone if that's the case. Besides, you have to be single, six feet tall, a high school graduate, not wear glasses, etcetera. I'm going to be a military police officer."

After he approved, in the background I heard one of my asshole brothers comment, "A what? A meathead?"

That was the beginning of my education in the field of law enforcement. Some people hate you, and some like you, but you can bet your ass they will listen to you when you speak.

No matter the event, family was there in good times and bad. Sometimes, as all teenagers do, I thought I was unloved and misunderstood by my parents. I was never a leader among my brothers. I was the willing follower though. I would try anything. If we got caught, the elder brother would face my parents' wrath. That probably was the most important lesson I learned in my young life: Be a leader, not a follower. Make your family proud. Be honest and just. Take your lumps when you deserve it, but never take shit from those who try to intimidate you. I recalled those lessons several times in my career.

"This is my job. I'm a good guy, and you're a bad guy. Do not try to intimidate me or my family, because I'm crazier than you are. If you take this personally, I will take it personally. If you threaten my family, I will threaten you, and then I will hurt your family. And if I can't do it, I have several friends in low places who will. I also have a few older brothers who are crazier than me." Crazy cop, I guess, but the attitude served me well. Most of the scum, including our friendly neighborhood one percenters, understood that philosophy. It was kill or be killed.

I'm a pretty no-nonsense, "you do the crime, and you do the time," kind of guy. Most bad guys understand and respect the game. They know that, as a result of their actions, they will have to face the music one day, and they take it. I like that kind of bad guy, honorable and professional. Those who say, "I know where you live, officer, and I'll get you back," don't really know who they are dealing with.

"You think Clint Eastwood is bad? Buddy, you ain't seen anything yet. Make my day? All right, I'll make your day, you mongoloid."

Nothing pleased me more than to see a big, tough drug trafficker, wife batterer, or simple murderer break down when confronted with damning evidence. It was better than sex.

I see myself as a friendly guy, somewhat naïve, and somewhat crazy. I like good Cape Breton scotch, my delicious homemade wine, and good people, and I dislike people who talk to me only when they want something. Over the years I have learned that if you do things for the right reasons, you will never regret it. You might fail sometimes, but if you try and do your best, life will be good.

On the particularly cold day when this adventure began, I was doing my thing when I answered that hellish telephone. "Bathurst Police, bonjour."

There was a pause. Then the voice on the other end said, "Oh, hello. I'm looking for Luc Landry."

"Speaking. What can I do for you, sir?"

Luc Landry was my cover name. I didn't tell anyone my real name until I knew to whom I was speaking.

"My name is Neal Jessop, and I work for the Windsor Police Service."

Holy shit! I thought. The president of the Canadian Police Association! Neal had done more for police officers across Canada than anyone I knew. He had the voice of a military sergeant major, which, right off the bat, impressed the hell out of me. I had been a good military guy once, and I was standing at attention as he spoke.

"I understand you're the contact person in New Brunswick on the CISO undercover police program, and I would like to talk to you about a case we have over here and see if you can help us out."

Again, CISO is an agency of the Ontario government, just as CISNB is an agency of the New Brunswick government. Like CISNB, CISO gathers and maintains intelligence on criminal activity in the province. The intelligence gathered includes information on criminal biker gangs and other organized crime activity. Its mandate is to ensure all police forces in Ontario are kept up to date on information about criminal activities in the province. It is also a conduit to all other police services in Canada and shares information with other criminal intelligence services. It is also well known in police circles as an excellent organization that conducts training in various aspects of police work, in particular, the undercover police operators program. It trains municipal, regional, and provincial police officers in the art of infiltration. As mentioned earlier, the Mounties do not allow undercover police training of municipal and regional police officers for reasons still unknown to me and all the other *real* cops in this country. I guess it has to do with tradition and the fear of losing the glory and press coverage on major cases in Canada.

When I think back to my training with CISO, it brings back sweet memories of a bunch of dedicated young men and women whose names will never be told, since some are still actively infiltrating criminal gangs. Like me, members of the Toronto police and regional services like Niagara regional, Hamilton regional, Peel regional police and, of course, the Ontario Provincial Police (OPP), are selected by their respective departments. After rigorous testing by CISO, they embark on a three-week training course that teaches good guys how to be bad guys—how to walk, how not to wear a seatbelt in a car, how to curse with the best of them, how to dress down or dress up, and how to rid themselves of inhibitions. Recruits must be confident in their ability to bullshit with the best. That always makes me smile, because one of my favorite sayings is, "If you can't dazzle them with brilliance, baffle them with bullshit."

The call from Neal Jessop was short and sweet. "I need a male UC, between thirty to forty years of age, a down homer who speaks French with the Acadian dialect of the Brayons of Grand Sault and Edmundston, NB. Can you help me out? We have a homicide here in Windsor, and we have suspects who reside in a crack house, some of whom are former down homers who now live in Windsor. They speak French. They're all from the Grand Sault area, and any UC will have to be able to communicate and understand the language in order to infiltrate this group. If you can find me a candidate, we'll have him come to Windsor and brief him on the basics of the incident. He'll also meet an agent who will assist in introducing him to the gang."

I informed him that a few officers fit the bill and that I would contact them to see if they were interested. Needless to say, not too many officers wanted to spend an unknown amount of time out of province, away from loved ones, to join a group of officers and handlers he did not know and, furthermore, to infiltrate a group of crackheads, one or two of which had murdered another crackhead.

I thought I was a perfect candidate, even though I was a bit older than Jessop wanted. I had been successful in all of my undercover operations from Tracadie to Caraquet, NB, from Edmundston to Bangor, Maine, from Halifax to God knows where. I had worked drugs, prostitoads, homicides, bootlegging, you name it. I believed that assholes in Ontario were just like assholes in New Brunswick. Infiltrating them would be the same, maybe a bit more difficult than what I was used to, but I was certainly gung-ho and cocky enough to try it.

I made a few telephone calls to other UCs in the province, but after I explained the incident, there are no takers.

Shit, man, great system, I thought. I was responsible for the pool of municipal officers in the province, and none of them wanted the job. It was embarrassing.

Secretly, I hoped I could convince Jessop that, even though I was a bit older, I could do the job. I had a feeling of excitement, as if I were an actor. For justice to be done, someone had to stick his neck out and make it happen. I honestly believe I had a mental problem, that I still do. Who in their right mind would do that shit? To be honest, UC officers are a little nutty. Like actors, they need the limelight, the glory, the adoration of their public. You can't be a good UC if you're not full of it.

That, I thought, *is no problem with me. I'm so full of it, it scares me.*

I believed that, like an actor, the public would admire me. My wife, my kids, and all of the other officers would be proud of me, and at the same time I would get to rid the world of a couple of murderers. Not bad for a little down homer to go to the big province and kick some serious derriere. The road to greatness started off made of gravel and then ended with beautiful black tar—in Ontario, of course.

So it began. I proposed to Neal that no one was interested in the job except me and that I would be happy to give it a shot. I don't know what he was thinking or what kind of pressure he was under, but, as a detective, I knew he was calling me as a last resort. They had tried everything, and nothing was happening. He needed to get things moving. This was Windsor, Ontario, a tunnel or bridge drive across from the most murderous city in the USA. How could Detroit have close to five hundred homicides a year while the city across the river, not one kilometer away, had only eight?

I didn't know what he was thinking, but I knew it was important to Neal that Windsor remain one of the safest cities in the country. He was a great man, no politician. No citizen knew how much he loved his city and his country. He was also a no-nonsense guy, just like me. I would protect my people or die trying. He could have been our prime minister, but he cared too much for his people, and when you care too much, you tend to suffer from PTSD (please try something different) for your people. He was a legend in Windsor police circles and a hero to every cop in this country, and I loved him.

Neal had exhausted all traditional methods of investigation. The suspect crew was a group of hardened, small-time crooks who, for the most part, had had several run-ins with the legal system and knew exactly what the cops could and could not do. Needless to say, none of them were talking. They were tight, and they were scared of the killer, who, apparently, was a raving lunatic who was stoned on crack half of the time and just plain stupid the rest of the time.

After some more discussion and approval from my police chief, Lloyd Armstrong, it was agreed that I would be seconded to the Windsor Police Service to try to infiltrate the crackhead group in the hope of obtaining information on who did the shooting, who helped dispose of the body, and who cleaned up the crime scene. It was a challenge, but I had faced some pretty long odds in other UC jobs and had been successful. This one was different though. No details were provided to ensure that my testimony in court would not be tarnished by what I might have heard in briefings and conversations with other cops. All I knew was that on Labor Day weekend 1997, the Windsor cops found a male body along a walking trail on the city's west side, and preliminary reports indicated he had been shot once in the head by an unknown caliber rifle or handgun. The identification of the victim pointed them toward the so-called West End gang. The victim was a small time crook who was addicted to dope and did minor crimes to support his habit. He was part of a small group of individuals who specialized in break and enters and any kind of scam possible. The victim and his buddies were all well known to the Windsor police.

Jessop and his capable team of investigators had tracked the group and deduced that the victim had been shot in the crack house at 921 Wellington Avenue in Windsor. It was rented by William "Billy" Murdock Mackenzie, a loud, ignorant, and abrasive individual who was a useless piece of shit. Billy was about five feet nine inches tall with reddish hair and a loud, scratchy voice. He had aspirations of being the godfather or Mom Boucher. Unfortunately, brain cells were not very plentiful in his gene pool. That didn't matter to Billy, because he had a bit more than his cronies.

Neal also advised me that his team had secured an agent who would introduce me to the rest of the West End gang. "I'll make arrangements for you to fly to Windsor, meet the troops, the agent, and the Iceman," Neal said.

"Okay, fine," I said. "I know I have to meet the agent and the troops, but who in hell is the Iceman?"

It turns out it was the nickname the cops had given to the local crown prosecutor. Great, as if there was not enough pressure already. Now I had to meet some guy who was probably as tough as nails. I imagined the meeting. He would look me up and down and say, "He's too old" or "I don't think he's going to be able to infiltrate this gang. After all, he's from down east, probably too much of a nice guy!"

Even if the nickname scared me a bit, I would be on my best and toughest behavior. I would project myself as a tough, non-commissioned officer sergeant in the military police. All military folks knew that if you wanted something done right, you got a sergeant to do it! The Iceman was probably like a colonel who was great with the paper pushing but had no idea what to do on the front lines. Once we talked, however, I was confident he would be satisfied with Neal's choice.

Sure enough, our first and only meeting with the Iceman went well. I noted that he was straightforward and direct, and I got the impression he was a no-nonsense person who had the same goal as the other cops and me—to get Ron Lougheed's killer.

"Once everyone knows each other, I want to ensure that you're comfortable with the agent and that he, of course, is comfortable with you," the Iceman said.

Fair enough. Police agents were a necessary evil. They weren't cops. They were bad guys who, for whatever reason, had decided to help the cops. In this case, my new partner was the owner of the vehicle that had been used to dispose of the body. He was of Acadian descent, spoke good French, and had a record for drug trafficking and some other shit I wasn't interested in hearing. He wasn't entirely convinced that I wouldn't shoot him or that his buddies wouldn't call him a rat for working with the cops. The charges against him were pretty heavy, since his car had been used to dump the body. No matter how many times he told the cops he was not aware they had used his car, his complaints fell on deaf ears. After he learned that being charged as an accessory to murder after the fact was a definite possibility, he saw the light and signed a contract for monetary return if and when the cops were able to arrest Lougheed's murderer.

I, the good guy, was not too confident that the agent was solid. Would he inform his lunatic friends that I was a cop? Would they put one in my head like they had to Lougheed? Was I scared? Should I have been? I would be covered by eight of Canada's top cops, and if they didn't get there in time, I could handle myself. If that didn't work, well, they'd be parading every September on Parliament Hill in my honor. I would be esteemed alongside my brother and sister officers who had fallen in the line of duty. That was a pretty good deal.

It was about that time that I understood I was a real cop. I was not afraid. I was going to Windsor to help my brother and sister officers, not solve a murder. They had asked for my help, and I was

Josh Ouellette

happy to oblige. I was not a hero, I was a cop, and any one of those guys would have done the same for our department. It was in my blood. It's hard to explain. Maybe it was the pursuit of justice for the weak. Maybe it was vanity, pride, but it sure felt good when it was successful and my brothers and sisters lifted a glass in my honor.

2

THE VISIT AND THE INTRODUCTION

I had obtained all of the required false identification, including driver's license, library card, social insurance number, and so on. Using my covert identification, I reserved a seat on our beloved Air Nova for Windsor with a pit stop in Montreal. I was dressed down in jeans, ball cap, cowboy boots, a shaved head, and three weeks' growth on my face.

After presenting my notice that I was an on-duty police officer, security gave me no hassle, even though I was carrying a weapon—a lethal and precise 9 mm Beretta handgun. I was to be picked up at the Windsor airport and transported to my hotel, where I would meet the team and my handlers. It would be the start of the long process of introductions, trust building, and endless hours of intelligence briefings and arguments.

It was clear to me immediately upon my arrival that Windsor was a beautiful city. It sat at the southernmost part of Canada's largest province and was a short drive across a bridge or tunnel to Detroit, one of America's most beautiful, yet dangerous, cities.

Cops in Windsor were the real thing. "Brother" and "sister" were terms the officers there used often, and they meant it! They were brothers and sisters. When I arrived in Windsor, I felt an uncanny energy from the team of men and women, who did not know how impressive they were. I felt special, and after hearing the term "brother" a few times, I was convinced that these guys and gals, from Neal on down, really were my brothers and sisters.

It's a strange thing, folks. No other profession, except maybe nursing or firefighting, makes a person feel that way about his or her peers. When you deal with despair, anger, innocence, and ignorance day in and day out, it's easy to understand why all of the first responders feel close to each other. No one knows what the hell they feel when they pick up a hurt kid or a battered women or an asshole druggie. Those people don't get the credit they deserve.

A uniformed female officer picked me up at the Windsor airport, and we exchanged pleasantries. She smiled and told me that she had been ordered to take me to the hotel where Neal would meet me.

After arriving at the hotel, I finally got to meet some of Canada's best cops: Neal, Jerome (Brags) Brannagan, Detective Kuzak, Sgt. Stibbs, and Cst. Green, our IT specialist. I had brought a couple of bottles of my homemade blueberry wine, so in no time, everyone felt relaxed. It was sixteen percent alcohol, close to cognac, so we became friends quickly, and I felt very comfortable with those guys. No games; I felt like they respected me, and I knew I respected them. We were going to do all right. They were my kind of people.

They briefed me on the job at hand. The plan was to introduce me to the suspects through the agent, Kenneth Legace. As I noted before, he was a transplanted down homer with an extensive criminal record whose car had been used to transport and dump Lougheed's body.

Ken was a petty criminal with a drug problem who had been involved with the West End gang for a long while. He had committed break and enters with Billy and the group and was no stranger to the police or their procedures. Ken was also a tough cookie who would never rat on a buddy, but after he realized he could be charged as an accessory to murder, a little friendly persuasion by the investigators led him to decide that working for the cops wasn't such a bad deal. All he needed to do is introduce me as an old friend from back home in Grand Sault, NB, and I would handle the rest. He would sign a contract with the police, get paid a certain amount for his time and services, and avoid charges. It was a good deal.

Ken swore that he was not present the night Lougheed was murdered and had not been told who committed the crime. He told the cops that all he knew was that there was a party, and Billy and Wahoo were involved in some way. Wahoo was an aboriginal guy, a big boy with an intimidating look in his eye.

Other than being a criminal, Ken was a pretty decent guy. He had a good family back home, and, as the story goes, he had come to the big city to find work but ended up with a bunch of losers, thereby becoming a loser himself. Neal told me that prior to final authorization of the operation, they needed to be certain he would be straight up and that he wouldn't blab that I was a cop as soon as the operation began. I felt good, because the guys cared about my safety, and it was obvious that Neal and the boys understood some level of trust had to exist between a UC and an agent. Otherwise, no progress would be made in the murder case, and most of their time would be spent checking out the agent so that he remained on the up and up. After a quick briefing, my handlers told me the agent was on his way to the hotel to meet me and have a chat.

As soon as I met Ken, it became apparent that he was smart and conniving. We introduced ourselves, and then I asked him about his hometown, telling him that I had several relatives still living there. I could tell he was impressed by my knowledge of the area, and he relaxed quickly. Our conversation was casual and polite. Ken's main concern was that I couldn't do the job and that his buddies would find out I was a cop and do something nasty to him. Meanwhile, I was concerned that he was untrustworthy and that he would tell his buddies I was a cop and they would do nasty things to me! I explained that I had been doing this type of work for many years and that he should not worry about me burning the case. He seemed satisfied with that. Thirty minutes later, he left the hotel room.

After Ken left, Neal asked me how I felt about him. Was I all right with the guy? Could I work with him? Could I trust him not to bullshit?

I explained to Neal that for the agent to open up and trust me, sometimes I would have to take his side over the cops. In all agent/UC relationships, there comes a time when the agent screws up or fails to do what was asked of him. He might feel scared, or regret ratting on his friends. At that point, the handlers have to jack him up, meaning bring him in and, in not so friendly terms, explain that they are not satisfied with his work and that they are just about ready to shut down the file and throw him in jail for failure to honor his contract. When that happens, the agent might complain to the UC, who will sympathize with him and try to help by talking to the handlers on his behalf. That serves to tighten the bond between the UC and the agent. It's the "you and me against them" syndrome, and it works.

That investigative technique proved to be very useful in this case. After a few rough days, Ken came on board and contributed fully to the investigation. All we told him was that I was Luc Landry from New Brunswick, that I was a cop, and that he had been hired to introduce me to his friends, who were suspects in the Ronald Lougheed homicide.

3

THE OPERATION BEGINS

On March 5, 1998, I met with Detectives Cliff Lovell and Dave Perpitch, two of the senior investigators in the Lougheed homicide. They handed me a copy of the authorization, which was dated March 4, 1998 and was valid until May 1, 1998. It was a legal document authorizing the police to intercept calls and communications between the subject of interest and me. It was known as "the wire."

It was 1998, so I didn't have any fancy gizmos or cameras attached to my shirt. I was provided with a flip phone that would be attached to my belt. The phone would serve as a transmitter to monitor and record all conversations to accumulate evidence or to alert the officers if I was in trouble or something big was going down. It was kind of weird, because I couldn't use the phone to send or receive calls. I was a little leery of that. They told me that if any of the bad guys asked to use it, I should just tell them the battery was dead. Hopefully, they wouldn't have a charger around. But I concluded I needed the phone to protect myself, so I would have to improvise if something came up. That was the part of the job that was scary yet motivating. It was also why they paid me the big bucks. I had no reason to believe there would be any dangerous incidents, so off we went.

At 1330 hours on March 5, 1998, I picked up Ken at his residence on Assumption Street in Windsor. We were to drive around town and get to know each other. He showed me the house at 921 Wellington Street, the location where the murder allegedly took place. It was the residence of William Murdock Mackenzie, who was the main target in the operation and one of the suspects believed to have murdered Lougheed. It is a decrepit, unkempt place. As I looked at it, I feel odd yet excited that things were moving along.

We spent the rest of the afternoon seeing the sights of Windsor. Ken was quite proud to show me the Hiram Walker plant and Riverside Drive, where the Freedom Festival was held each year. Along the way, he wanted to visit a possible customer who needed a new roof. The gentleman told him he wanted the job done later.

As we were leaving the house, Ken pointed to the back of the old guy's house. "That's where they found the body," he said.

We spent the remainder of the afternoon getting to know each other and getting our cover story straight so that, if questioned, our story would jive. We stopped at Gilligan's Burgers and worked out the details over lunch.

"I've just arrived from New Brunswick, and while looking for a room and lunch, I stopped at the Allouette Club," I said. "While sipping my beer, I saw you and started shooting the breeze about everything—the weather, the city, and, of course, where I'm from and where you're from. You told me that you were originally from Grand Falls, NB, and I told you that I was from Beresford.

"At that point, I let you know that I spent my first years of school in Grand Falls. After a bit more conversation and a few more beers, we recognized each other as old schoolmates. I could not have been happier to meet someone in Windsor who could help me find a job and start a new life. I lost my job as a janitor at the Chaleur Regional Hospital back home in Bathurst, and my wife kicked me out because of my drug abuse problem. So it's reasonable to assume that I'm in bad shape, a loser, and, that like many down homers, I've come to the big province to start over, find a good job, maybe a girlfriend, and try to straighten myself out."

I emphasized that I did not take drugs of any kind except beer or hard stuff. Establishing the scenario of a recovering dope addict was necessary and important. Then I could refuse a toke or a hit when the targets offered me a joint or some coke. "No thanks, I'm off that shit," I'd say. "I lost everything back home, and I don't want to screw up anymore. I'll just sit here and drink my beer. No dope for me, but thanks anyway." The story was something the suspects would accept without a doubt, since they didn't like to share their stuff anyway.

By the way, undercover cops *do not* break the law to obtain evidence and then use that evidence to convict someone else who has broken the law. Taking illegal drugs is a criminal act, and there are many other ways to show a target that you are a bad guy without using drugs. In my numerous undercover operations, big and small, I never used any kind of illegal drugs, and I never committed a criminal act. I was never really challenged about my life story either. I was proud of that. I was also proud that I could enter any world and be accepted by everyone. I always thought it was my big, blue eyes or my lively conversations that endeared me to my targets, but the truth is, they didn't really give a shit. Those who know me know that bullshitting is one of my strongest traits. I suppose my appearance was another factor. I measured 5 feet, 9 inches and weighed 196 pounds at the time and had a beer gut, a shaved head, and no teeth. That probably went a long way toward convincing the bad guys that I was not a cop.

In training, our instructors at the CISO course told us we had to blend in and not be noticed, unless we wanted to substantiate our cover story. In other words, we shouldn't wear $300 dollar cowboy boots when infiltrating a bunch of losers who had trouble affording sneakers, and we shouldn't wear a shirt and tie unless we were crashing a wedding. All of those details had to be taken into consideration if we want to be accepted. At times, it was hard to separate fact from reality, since I thought it was exciting to play a part, be an actor, and convince others that I was someone else.

On this particular case, I wanted to portray a loser, a recovering drug addict, a nice guy who was trying to move on with life. It was working. I felt that Ken accepted me, and that meant his friends would also accept me eventually and open up. I had to help the boys solve a homicide. I liked the Windsor cops. They had their community at heart. To them, it was not a job, it was a vocation. They were my kind of cops, doing it for the right reasons.

After our long conversation, Ken and I were satisfied that our cover story was strong and that things would work out in the end for everyone involved. We left Gilligan's, and I dropped Ken off at his residence. Then I returned to the safe house, where I did a debriefing with my handlers, spin team members, and investigators. The safe house was the opposite of the dump house. It was where I would reside when I was off duty, getting some down time away from the bad guys. I would also use it for meetings with handlers and so on. The Windsor boys had set me up in a downtown hotel, which was perfect. It was far enough away from the target, and there was no chance that any of them would be in that part of town.

By the way, the spin team was made up of Windsor police officers who followed me around and ensured my protection. They did a lot of U-turns, slow driving, or fast driving to get in a good position to keep an eye on their target. I suppose all that fancy driving was why they were called the "spin team." They were always moving around but not really going anywhere. In addition to protection, the spin team identified people I didn't know and gathered intelligence when possible. Those guys were good. I never noticed anyone following us. I knew they were there, but I never saw them. I was confident they had my back though, which was a good feeling.

After that first day, I felt a lot better. Things were moving along steadily and safely with the agent and the cops, and I was confident I had the qualities to convince the killer to open up to me and, hopefully, confess to the crime.

4

MY FIRST MEETING WITH BILLY

March 6, 1998. That's the day Ken introduced me to his friends and suspects. It was an extremely important moment to confirm their acceptance of me and my cover story.

As I walked up the stairs to Ken's apartment, I crossed paths with a woman who had long, brown hair and was about five feet, five inches tall. When I asked her if Ken was home, she replied rather brusquely that he was upstairs and then kept on walking. She was pissed off at either Ken or me. I figured that either she knew I was a cop and was upset about it or she was upset with Ken for inviting assholes to her apartment. Probably the latter, seeing as she was not supposed to know that he was working with the police. Love is grand!

Our plan for the day was to drop in at Billy's place to see if Ken had any mail there. Apparently, he got his mail delivered to Billy's place and picked it up on a regular basis. I was to accompany my long-lost friend for a quick intro to the target.

We made few stops along the way—at the dry cleaners to pick up pants and then at a small convenience store, where Ken was trying to find a client who needed a roofing job, to no avail.

We arrived at Billy's place, and I stood beside Ken when he knocked on the door. A white male answered. I knew it was Billy. I recognized him from the photos the Windsor boys had shown me earlier. Ken introduced me matter of factly as his buddy from down east and asked Billy about his mail. Billy told him there was none and that, in the future, he should call before coming over. They exchanged a few more words about nothing, and then Ken and I left.

On our way out the door, Ken told Billy that we would be going for a beer later and that he was welcome to join us. Billy agreed, so Ken told him that we would be back later to pick him up.

We headed for the Allouette Club, where Ken lamented about his girlfriend problems. We also discussed what the approach would be when we returned to Billy's house.

At about 1500 hours, we leave the Allouette Club and stopped at a beer store, where I bought a twelve pack. Then we proceeded to Billy's house for a visit and a bit of introductory conversation.

Billy was a white male, 35–40 years of age, 5 foot 9 inches tall, 160 pounds, with short blonde/brown hair, a long goatee, white-rimmed glasses, blue eyes, bottom teeth missing, a tattoo of a spider's web on his left elbow, a small hole on the left side of his forehead, and a scar on the left side of his stomach. When I met him, he was wearing jeans and a red-and-white sports shirt that was torn under the right forearm. He was a loud and abrasive person. Every second word was a swear word, and that's putting it lightly.

When we arrived, Billy let us into the kitchen area, which was somewhat messy. I would probably describe it as a hoarder's house. Small air conditioning units, clothes, boots, dishes—you name it, it was strewn all over the place.

Billy moved some of the clothes and stuff off the small kitchen table and chairs so we could sit down and chat. Most of the conversation was between Ken and Billy. It centered around one of their buddies, who owed both of them some money and whom they had not seen around for a while. They also talked about the weather and something about Ken's tools that were stored at Billy's house. I didn't say much, just listened and ensured that I memorized everything about that little house, Billy, and any other information that might be pertinent to the case so that I could complete my notes as precisely as possible. I was sure that the boys had taken photos and sketches of the crime scene and anything else pertaining to the shooting, but I needed to gather the information for myself for my testimony later in court. It was also important for me to figure out the quick exits from the house in case some fool picked up a gun or something.

To the left of the main entrance, I noted a blanket covering what I assumed was a doorway to another room, probably the living room. I knew I would be permitted inside eventually. According to Billy, the blanket was to keep the warmth in, but I was convinced that some activities or persons were in that room that Billy did not want casual visitors, like me, to see.

The conversation went on until Ken went to use the washroom. While he was gone, Billy and I chatted about how weird it was that Ken and I had run into each other, especially after such a long time. I told him about our chit chat at the Allouette Club, and he seemed to buy the story, which he had heard already from his longtime buddy. So far, so good.

When Ken returned, he told Billy that I had left my car parked on the street a little farther up from his house. That way the neighbors couldn't see my car and wouldn't gossip about the cops being at

Billy's house again. I didn't understand why Ken said that, but later I learned that the vehicle I was driving looked like an unmarked police car. How right they were.

Prior to my arrival in Windsor, I had inquired about wheels for the operation. Should I take an unmarked unit from home or rent one in Windsor? After a short conversation with Neil and Brags, we decided I should bring a couple of New Brunswick license plates, registration papers, and so on. The Windsor police would supply the vehicle, I'd put the plates on it, and no one would be the wiser—or so I hoped. However, on my first visit to Billy's place, someone had commented that my car looked an awful lot like a police car. That explained why Ken had insisted that I park a little farther up the street so as not to spook Billy and his friends.

My car was quite a common vehicle used all across Canada by cops and regular folks, so there was no reason to believe that Billy and the boys would make anything of it. However, when stressed out about something like being a suspect in a murder, people tend to be a little more paranoid and see cops everywhere—on the street, in cars, in their nightmares, and especially in their hallucinations when under the influence of garbage drugs. All that to say, Billy was happy we had parked a little farther up the street.

The conversation continued, with Billy saying that he hadn't seen the cops for about three weeks and that his place was probably bugged with cameras and microphones. Both Billy and Ken looked up at the wall and laughed. I didn't get the joke, so I asked Billy what was going on. He explained that the cops had arrived at his place and told him a murder had taken place there and that he had to leave until further notice so they could do a crime scene investigation.

He had been locked out of his place for three weeks. When he returned, he found that they had cut out part of the floor, which he indicated by pointing to the part of the floor where the tile had been removed. I saw what appeared to be a small hole. He also showed me dark spots on the ceiling that, according to the cops, were bloodstains. He added that the so-called murder had happened back in August or September of the previous year. He was very talkative, and by his demeanor, he seemed quite comfortable talking about it with me.

"Did you know the guy?" I asked. "Was he a friend?"

"No, not a friend," he replied. "He was here quite a bit though, because this was a party place."

Billy fell silent, like he was remembering something or was afraid he was talking too much to someone he had just met. I didn't pursue the topic, and we continued talking, with Billy informing me of places where I could probably could get a job in the city.

I talked about other friends, and then he told me he had a good friend who was an Indian but did not have his status card. I said that that was too bad, because, with the price smokes cost me back home in NB, if his buddy had his card, I could buy cigarettes tax-free from him in Ontario, return to sell them in New Brunswick, and make a big profit. That way I wouldn't have to find a job, just smuggle the smokes back home and live well.

Billy didn't mention his Indian friend's name, but I assumed he was talking about Wahoo, our second target. I didn't pursue the matter for fear of showing too much interest in Wahoo and creating some doubt in his mind about me. I didn't want him wondering why, on the first day he met me, I wanted to know his life story. I figured it would be safer to let him to bring up Wahoo whenever he wanted. I needed to appear like a follower. Let him speak and let him tell me what to do, if need be. I had to gain his confidence, and the only way I could do that was by letting him speak, build his confidence as a leader of the packrats, and never argue about a subject I was not supposed to know anything about, like how to kill someone. I was to ensure that Billy and his buddies saw me as nothing more than a down homer looking for a job in the janitor business anywhere around town.

It was a fine line though. If I showed that I was nothing but a follower and a wimp, they would take advantage of me. The group was like a pack of dogs with their "Alpha Bill" leader who would either sniff my ass and accept me or beat the shit out of me. Those boys needed to know that even though I was quiet and a nice guy, I wouldn't take crap from anyone. I would fight back with my gift of the gab first and then throw a couple of punches and kicks if need be. That served to calm everyone in most cases, but not when people were flying on cheap meth or coke.

A short while later, I asked Billy where I could get smokes. I left Ken behind and went to pick up a pack. At that time, they were without a doubt talking about me. Billy was probably questioning Ken about who the hell I was and so on. When I returned, I would observe any changes in conversation, eye contact, or lack thereof and any other signs that would help me get Lougheed's killer.

Back at the house, everything seemed unchanged, and the conversation continued until Ken told Billy we had to go. I opened my new pack of smokes and handed one to both of them as I lit up. While walking to the door, Billy asked if he could get

Josh Ouellette

an extra one for later. I opened the pack and handed over half of it.

"Thanks for your help, Billy, about the job hunt."

I left the house a little worried that my act of kindness might come back to bite me on the ass. Who in his right mind handed over half a pack of smokes and didn't ask for anything in return? I was a little worried that I had overdone the "good guy" stuff until I concluded that perhaps Billy believed I was just a good down homer, friendly and helpful. Surely Billy would know that a cop would never hand over something as valuable as cigarettes to a lowlife like him.

After dropping Ken at his residence, I met up with the handlers for our daily debriefing.

I also did a lot of soul searching at that time. Was I doing well? How were my wife and kids back home? It was expected that I would doubt myself, that I would think too much about my feelings, and so on, but I had to shake it off.

"Be cool," I told myself. "Suck it up, and be tough. You can handle it."

All was well, I believed. All we needed was patience, and things would fall into place. I was being careful. I had gauged those guys pretty well and did not feel any kind of opposition or distrust from Billy, and I hoped that would continue. It was only a matter of time before Billy or one of his cohorts would mouth off about the murder or try to impress me with what a big, bad criminal they were. I believed the operation was proceeding well so far and that I had to be patient. There was no pressure from Neal or the other cops to get it done quickly, which made me feel good. The pressure would be bad enough just hanging with Ken and Billy. I didn't want my handlers to get impatient on top of that. Pushing for information was stressful. I never knew what the target's reaction would be, and doing so could sabotage the investigative process and, more importantly, could become rather unhealthy for me.

At the safe house, I had a good, strong shot of rum and relaxed. I was doing well, and I would continue to do well. My wife and kids would be proud. I would show the big city cops that we down homers could be trusted to do a good job. A lot was riding on the case. I was a proud Acadian cop and would do everything possible to bring justice to Ronald Lougheed's family.

5

QUESTIONS ABOUT MY COVER STORY

The following day, at about 0900 hours, I met up with the handlers at the safe house, and they gave me a transcript of the conversation between Billy and Ken that had transpired while I was not present the previous day. The recording was obtained through wiretap or transmitters in Billy's house and phone.

The transcript of the conversation between Billy and Ken revealed that they were comfortable with me around, and there were no indications that Billy doubted my story. More importantly, it confirmed that Ken as being straight up with the other cops and me.

At about 1350 hours, I pick up Ken at his apartment. I informed him that we would drop in to see Billy and only stay for a few minutes. Before going there, we stopped at a small sports bar and ordered a beer. While chatting, I told Ken that I would be out of town for the weekend and that we would get at it again the following week. He didn't like that and complained that I hadn't given him any money, and neither had the cops. I called the office and spoke with Kim, our IT tech, and told him about the situation and that I would give Ken twenty bucks to keep him quiet until more funds for him could be arranged. I added that it was probably time to meet with Neal and the boys and set things straight so that Ken and I understood what was expected of us.

We left the bar and stopped at the local beer store, where I gave Ken fifty bucks to get some beer for our afternoon visit to Billy's place.

At Billy's, we parked a short distance away. The parking spot that Ken suggested I use was a gravel alleyway along a railway track at the back of the house. It was off the street, but it was not quite hidden. The only people who couldn't see the car were Billy's front neighbors. Ah well, so be it.

Ken went to the door, did the secret knock, and went in while I waited at a picnic table in the backyard with the case of beer. A few minutes later, Ken came out, followed by Billy, another man identified later as Pat "Trashcan" Mackenzie (Billy's brother), and a big goon named Norm Plourde.

The conversation with a cold beer in hand was cordial, but I got the distinct impression the two strangers were checking me out. They were a little hyper, walking around me, staring at me, and not saying anything. Something was going on, and I figured it was Billy's way of introducing me to a few of his buddies to get their opinion of me.

At one point, Ken spoke to Norm in French, and then it dawned on me that the guy was probably checking out my language abilities, accent, and so on. Norm seemed like a likeable guy, and on his first word to me, I detected a good, old Brayon accent.

Brayon is French and a derivative of Acadian ancestry, which is spoken commonly in northwestern New Brunswick. On the other side of the province, where I come from, there is less slang when locals speak French, while in southeastern New Brunswick, they have the dialect known locally as "Chiac." Even I can't understand it fully because of the way they mix French and English syllables in the same word.

It's easy for me to understand why such a small province has so many different accents and slang words. Languages and dialects in New Brunswick were influenced by Canada's history. First, the French landed in the coastal regions of Eastern Canada, called the place "Acadie" and settled as fisherman, lumberjacks, and so on. Others settled further north. Things went well for a while until the Brits came along and took over all of the coastal areas. They continued towards Quebec but were unable to conquer that province. Later, the French and the English signed a treaty to keep out of each other's hair. Unfortunately, Acadians who spoke French had to learn English and swear allegiance to the British monarchy. That was where the problems began.

Most of the Acadians who refused to swear allegiance were put on ships and sent back to France. Those who did not want to go back to France moved to Quebec, eastern New Brunswick, the west side of New Brunswick, and even to the United States, especially Louisiana. It was obvious that Acadians would have to learn English, because they were a British colony. Hence the different dialects: "Chiac," in southeastern New Brunswick, "Brayon" in northwestern New Brunswick, Scottish English in southern New Brunswick, and Quebec French in eastern New Brunswick, where I'm from. It's a little confusing, but anyone who originates from New Brunswick can tell what part of the province a person is from.

It became clear to me that my visit to Billy's place and Norm's presence was to determine if I was a Brayon, a Chiac, or a French guy from northern New Brunswick. There was no doubt that Norm was from Grand Sault, the same area where Ken was from, and when I told him as much, he seemed to be satisfied and impressed with me and my knowledge of his hometown. Trashcan, on the other hand, was just there to be there. He was harmless, a bit drunk and a bit mouthy like his younger brother, Billy.

After a while, I informed everyone that I was headed out to Niagara Falls to visit my brother-in-law and I'd see them later. "Keep the rest of the beer, boys," I said. "I'll see you guys next week."

I returned to the safe house, where I met Brags and Kim. After a short debriefing, I was done for the weekend. A long weekend was coming up, and I was looking forward to it.

Later that evening, I jumped into my car and headed to St. Catherine's, not Niagara Falls, but I did actually visit my brother-in-law and his family, along with my son, who was studying at Brock University.

It was quite easy to hide my identity and my job from the bad guys, but how could I explain it to my family? They had seen me many times over the years working on various cases for their local police, so they didn't ask me too many questions, especially since they believed I was there to see my son. I spent an enjoyable weekend with my son's buddies and my in-laws and then headed back to the safe house in Windsor on Monday night to prepare for another week of intense activities.

When I arrived in Windsor, I checked in with Brags to see if anything was going on. I was surprised and a little worried when he ordered me to stay at the safe house and not go anywhere until he talked to me. Apparently, they had received information from the wire, and Brags wanted me to make a decision. He called back and told me to go to the station. He would let me in the back door.

I proceeded to the station, where Braggs told me he wanted to play the tape and see what I made of it. It became evident quickly that there had been a party at Billy's place, and the guests were a little drunk or stoned and some fights had broken out. There was also, as expected, a lot of chatter about the new French guy from down east. I heard Billy saying to unknown persons, "This guy is a cop. Let's kill him, take and sell his car, and no one will be the wiser." I overheard Ken saying, "He is not a cop," but that's about it. He did not defend me like I thought he would, and he certainly did not try to dissuade Billy from killing me. Other than the drunken rant, the cops hadn't obtained any other useful information.

As I wrote earlier, if a person was new to a place, was introduced as a long-lost friend, bought some beer, and then left, any normal human being would make a comment after the subject left. We all do it. Humans are like that. If they like or dislike you, they will certainly not say it to you, but you can bet you will be the subject of conversation once you leave the room. These guys were no different except that they were drunk or stoned, a little bit crazier, and they were already aware of and involved in the murder of another person. The question was, were they serious about killing me or were they just drunk and being stupid? Should we shut down the operation because of the possibility those assholes would make good on their drunken rant, or was it just the booze talking? Needless to say, I was a bit concerned and so were the other investigators.

I thought long and hard about what to do, and they gave me the choice to shut down the operation if I thought the comments were serious. It wasn't easy. There was no way I wanted to give up on the case. Call it what you want—ego, stupidity, or dedication—but I was not ready to drop everything and flee. Undercover cops, as I said earlier, are a bit crazy themselves. They can't let themselves be intimidated, because that's what bad guys do. Billy might have thought he was the alpha male, and I let them believe that, but in my mind, I was a pit bull, a smarter pit bull. I was not afraid. I would have to be more careful, not turn my back on any of them, and not get drunk and stupid like them. If they were going to do me in, they would have to be smarter, faster, and sober, and they would have to face one crazy mother. At the time, I was convinced I was superior to them on all fronts. I was that cocky, probably stupid, but there was no way I was going home with my tail between my legs, and I would not surrender to threats from those low lives. What would the Windsor cops think? What about the Bathurst cops? Worse, what would my family think?

All my wife and kids knew was that I working in Ontario, but they didn't question me about the specifics. I was happy that they were not aware of the details. All they knew was that their dad was a policeman, a good guy, and he put bad guys away. At least I think that's all they knew.

Then there were my brothers! Six of my brothers and I had served in Canada's armed forces at one time or another—two in the air force, one in the navy, three in the army, and one in the American army. I was confident that, should some scum from Windsor hurt their little brother, one of my brothers would make a quiet visit to the city for recon and then return to New Brunswick, where a family holiday would be planned to visit that wonderful part of southern Ontario. You think the Italian families are bad, well, you haven't seen my Acadian brothers. We had all of the bases covered: a couple of air force guys for comms, two infantry men from the well-known and respected Royal Canadian Regiment (RCR) and the Royal 22nd Regiment (Vandoos) for ground search and destroy, and our younger brother, the navy guy, for body disposal in Lake Ontario. My older brother, who was an American soldier, would be sitting on the shores of Detroit with a bottle of Moosehead beer or Bacardi rum should we encounter any flak from the Yanks. You get the idea. I could intimidate, too!

Many a man has died honorably for something in which he believes. We search for love and recognition, for respect from our peers, and, most importantly, self-respect. Honor. It's important to all men. I wondered often how many of my UC buddies would have loved to be there working such a big case in Windsor.

Brags wanted me to consider shutting it down. I felt that he was sincere and was concerned about my well-being. There was no way I would let those guys down though. After thinking about it for a few minutes, I informed them that I had no plans to give up on the case and that I was willing to continue to the best of my ability.

The conversation in which my life had been threatened had been taped on Friday night. My low life friends had been partying since I left at about two on Friday afternoon, and they had partied all weekend. It was important for me to know the exact time and the targets' state of mind when the threatening words had been stated. Brags informed me that they were all stoned and drunk and that the tape showed that it had been past midnight. I informed him and the troops that I would continue the operation on one condition: that I would never have to hang with those fools past ten at night. I believed that they were binge drinkers. Once started, they wouldn't stop. I thought that the possibility of them getting drunk, stoned, and crazy was higher late at night, so it was safer not to be there. Neal, Brags, and the boys were okay with my request, and we decided that the games would go on.

I felt good. I would have to be more alert, and I would have to keep an eye on my so-called buddy, Ken. He had lost my trust, and I felt silly. I was such a naïve individual. I hated myself when I thought that, but then again, it was part of my upbringing. "You are my friend until you prove me wrong" was another of my down home sayings. The moment I heard that tape, Ken was no longer my friend. He was a paid agent, a crook, an employee who was supposed to make it easier for me to get Lougheed's killer, and now I knew I had to use him to reach my goal. He was trying to cover his ass, get paid, get the cops to drop charges on him, and, hopefully, continue his loser life. It meant a little more stress, but, like I said, that's why I got paid the big bucks.

Several cases in my police career involved agents. Agents are not police informants. They are hired by police for their knowledge of incidents, suspects, and so forth. They are criminals themselves, but for whatever reason, they help the police infiltrate target organizations. Police investigators approach such individuals and, with a bit of leverage or money, convince them to turn on their criminal friends. After being told the rules, they sign a contract that obliges them to abide by their handler's orders. If successful, they receive their compensation and, depending on the crime and the criminal organization that might seek retribution against them, the police might move the agent to a new town to start a new life under a new identity, in addition to giving him or her money and some help finding a job. That task is a federal responsibility, so the RCMP is called in to assist with relocation and everything involved with that.

In our case, I was not aware of what would happen to Ken afterwards. It was not my responsibility, and I didn't care either. It was always in the back of my mind that if he could turn on his old friends, he could turn on me. It was a concern, but I had complete confidence in the Windsor boys, and I knew they would protect me and inform me if they had any doubts about Ken's loyalty. Brags's call confirmed that to me. They were keeping a close eye on Ken and his activities and, in turn, they would let me know about any serious incidents that could pose a threat. So, on we went. New procedures: Do not trust Ken, watch your ass, do not go to Billy's place after ten at night under any circumstances, and relax. Life was good.

At 0900 hours on the March 10, I proceeded to Ken's apartment for our daily activities. We headed to the social services office first so he could check on his welfare check, and then off we went to the local courthouse. We entered courtroom number five, and Ken's lawyer approached. After a short conversation, the court opened, and the lawyer informed the judge that his client wished to discharge him, because he was not satisfied. The judge accepted the lawyer's request for discharge and advised Ken that his date for trial was adjourned until April and that he had better have a lawyer present at that time to get on with his charges of drug trafficking. Ken agreed, and we left the courthouse to go for breakfast.

At the diner, I asked him about his weekend. "How did it go after I left them Friday?"

He said that all went well, that they had returned to the beer store for another case of beer and continued the party until about 0100 hours on Saturday morning. I questioned him, and he said there was a lot of bitching and complaining, that some of them didn't trust me. They thought I was a cop, and he did not make any great effort to contradict them. He added that he had stated, "He could be a cop, but I don't think so. He's cool, don't worry about it."

He also added that he had difficulty helping with my cover story, since they were asking him why I had shown up all of a sudden with money, a car that

Josh Ouellette

looked like a cop car, and so on. It became evident that Ken was not sticking his neck out to convince anyone that I was not a cop, that he certainly would not go to bat for me, because he was afraid for his own well-being. However, I felt that there was minimal danger for me and that the boys and I should come up with some scenarios to validate my identity with the guys, especially Billy. He was the most boisterous and mouthy individual in the gang. He talked a lot in an effort to impress his pals and me and appeared to be the leader of the rats. We agreed that we should hold a meeting with Neal and the boys to discuss the situation.

After supper, I picked up Ken at his apartment, and we drove to the Casa Don Motel on Cabana Road in Windsor. We had arranged for Neal and the handlers to be there. I had set up the meeting, because Ken was whining that he had no money. The cops were not giving him any, and he was upset about it. I had told Neal that it would be the ideal time to "jack us up," basically, to give us both shit for not getting anything done. It would serve the purpose of straightening Ken out and show him that Neal was the boss of him *and* me. Misery likes company, and I hoped that Ken would feel bad for me and would be more open as a result.

The plan was a success. Neil came in, and with his deep voice, explained to Ken that he would get his pay when and only when the job was done to Neal's satisfaction. "You two dickheads, get your act together and do the job!" Neal shouted, or words to that effect. His performance impressed the hell out of me.

I can assure you that it had the anticipated effect on my buddy as well. As Neal chastised us, I noted that Kem had a meek look on his face and that he regretted complaining about the cops not giving him funds. I was impressed by Neal's performance and thanked my lucky stars that I was on his side.

Following the "friendly debrief," we discussed the situation of Billy and his crew not being quite convinced of my identity. I told Neal that nobody would open up to me unless my cover was solid. I had to prove to them that I was and could be as bad as they were.

Renting a motel room as a "dump house" was a great start. Then I could invite Billy and whoever else to my place, and it would make it easier to have a conversation with just a few people about his involvement in the homicide. Billy's house was all wired up, and it made it easy for police to know what was up, but as I had said earlier to Neal, "They're all talking about Lougheed's death, but I can't get specifics from anyone, because there's always a half dozen people in various states of sobriety in the house." No names were ever mentioned in terms of who was responsible, and I was starting to think it might be a waste of time. The dump house would allow me to converse with Billy on a one-on-one basis and would serve as proof to Billy that I didn't have money, that I was just another nice guy from down east who spent all his money on buying his friends some beer but lived in a hole. I thought I was doing everything I had been trained to do, including appearance, dress, deportment, and so forth. I thought I looked like hell, which was perfect for my new friends. I had taken out my dentures, shaved my head, grown a dirty beard, and my clothes were not at all the latest fashion, but it all seemed to be useless. They did not trust me, and that was it. I had to do something to ensure that they saw me as a bad guy, one of them. The dump house served that purpose. Neal agreed, but the place would have to be wired up before anything went on there.

The following morning, Ken "Winnie" Green, our IT guy, ensured us that all required transmission devices would be installed. He was good at it! The interception of conversations from phones or from transmitters hidden in various rooms, vehicles, and so on require a possible covert entry, with a signed warrant, of course, and was probably the most technical part of the job. Conversations were recorded and, in turn, investigators listened to them and then had the conversations transcribed if they were related to the case. It was tedious work, and not everyone was suited to it. Not only did they have to try to understand what a drunken killer had said, they also had to write it down to the best of their ability, because the conversation could be used as evidence down the road. I did not envy the folks who were doing that on my case, simply because I couldn't even understand Billy when he was standing right in front of me. How the hell could those folks decipher what he was saying over the telephone?

In no time, the room was set, and the transmitters were activated, should someone come to visit. Conversations related to the case and under the authority of the judge's order could and would be recorded and transcribed for the investigators and, of course, the trial, should it ever come to that.

At about 1340 hours on March 11, I proceeded to Ken's apartment to pick him up with the intention of visiting Billy again to solidify my cover story. Unfortunately, Ken informed me that he was having some problems with his girlfriend and had to patch things up before going anywhere.

"Besides," he added, "Billy partied hard last night, and he won't be up to having company."

During our conversation, Ken also told me that he had heard from someone he did not want to identify that the weapon used to kill Lougheed was a .22 caliber rifle that used to belong to a deceased former Windsor police officer. Either Wahoo or another member of the West End gang had taken it recently from the son of the deceased officer. Acting like the resident forensic analyst, Ken told me that if the cops had already found the bullet in the wall or floor of Billy's house, they could easily confirm that the gun stolen from the deceased officer's son was the same one discharged in Billy's house and that it had been used to kill Lougheed.

I thought it was great news, except for the fact my friendly agent did not want to divulge who had told him that or where the gun was located. It was certainly an important piece of information, and I could understand why he would not tell me who had passed it on to to him, but I insisted that he tell me and that I would relay the info to the detectives. He said he had to call Scuza a little later and that he would relay the info himself. I could only surmise that Ken was worried that I would take credit for uncovering the evidence, thus depriving him of accolades and cuddles from the big, bad sergeant major. Our little face-to-face "jack up" with Neal at the motel a few days earlier had already produced a more focused agent. The plan was for him to trust me more and open up to me, because we were both getting heck from Neal for not producing enough, but in Ken's mind, I had become his competition rather than his buddy. Therefore, he wanted to keep the name of his source until he could tell Scuza himself. I giggled to myself and told him that it was all right but insisted that he pass the information on to the investigators as soon as possible, because it was important.

As Ken talked and talked, I could tell he was not at all motivated to go to work that day. I left, saying I would tell the cops about his info and that someone would call him at home.

I proceeded to the safe house, where I met with Neal, Scuza, and my cover team. I learned from Scuza that Ken was not being up front, that he did not want to work the case that day, because he had money and could party. We decided I should go back to the apartment and jack him up.

I returned to Ken's and started off by asking him what the hell was going on, that I had just got heck again from Neal. I told him that I was no longer his buddy, that he would do as I said, ask no questions, and get to the bottom of this so we could both get on with our lives. I added that I did not want to fail and go back to New Brunswick with my tail between my legs. The conversation got heated, and he raised his voice.

"What the hell do they want from me?" he asked. "The cops don't know what they're doing."

I put my hand up to stop his rant and then told him quickly and quietly that we were going to do what we had to do and get this shit over with. He was stubborn, but he understood.

As I continued to raise my voice, he put his finger to his lips and pointed upstairs, where I understood his girlfriend was. I reiterated that he had to be up front with me or else nothing would happen.

It was obvious that he was struggling. He did not like cops, he never had, and now he was hanging around with a cop and forced to say and do things that his criminal mind and attitude could not absorb. I guessed it was hard for him to do, but I was not the type of guy who put up with whining and complaining from an individual who sold drugs to kids and did everything in his power to hold back information from the police on a cowardly act of murder of another human being. I advised him that I would pick him up the next day at noon and that he had better be ready to go to work.

As I turned to leave, he asked me for my room number at the Casa Loma so that he could come by for a visit that night. I gave it to him, but, not surprisingly, he did not show up. Stress and fatigue was starting to get to him. Truthfully, I was starting to get a little pissed off with his complaining about this and that, and I had no more sympathy or patience for his tough life and miserable upbringing.

Holy shit, this guy is getting to me, I thought. *Be cool, and be professional. He's a loser in a bind, and you have to remain calm, organized, and firm. He'll use any means to get this over quickly.*

Later, I reminded Ken that quick was good, but that being on the up and up was essential if Billy was to answer for his crime. Ken, I learned, did not care about Billy, Lougheed, or anyone else. He cared about just one thing: himself. I would have to be cognizant of that. I could not trust him with my well-being. Not all criminals are bad people, and most bad people are not criminals. However, I was starting to believe that Ken was a product of the West End gang, that he was a criminal, and that he was a bad person. Consequently, I could not trust him, and I could not be nice to him, since he would use me, or anyone else, for that matter, to advance his cause, get away with criminal charges, make money, or to return to his wonderful life in the drug business. Was he a loser or merely a lost person? I didn't give a shit.

"Do the job, my friend, or I will make sure that you continue your loser life behind bars for a few years," I told him. I had to be the motivator to get the job done. I didn't need to panic. It would work out with Ken, and we would get Billy eventually.

I was starting to be concerned though. The information I had obtained was that two possible suspects were involved in Lougheed's murder, and so far, I had not even succeeded in believing that my cover was intact, at least in terms of Billy. At the rate things were going, the operation would last for a while. What concerned me was that police forces wanted to get the job done, but when the almighty dollar became an issue, there is a lot more stress on the investigators who, in turn, tried not to stress out the UC but, nevertheless, did it anyway. Everyone was worried about doing a good job. The investigators didn't want to disappoint me, and I didn't want to disappoint them. They were polite, and so was I. We tended to protect each other and, in my opinion, that could be dangerous. We had to be honest and up front with each other instead. As I told myself often, "Take your time, don't panic, things will pick up."

6
LUC "THE ROOFER"

At about 1200 hours on March 12, I went to help Ken and Billy do a roofing job. I was not a contractor, a carpenter, or anything close to a laborer type. I had advised Ken of that, so he told me that he would make sure I wouldn't embarrass myself or fall off the roof or anything like that. It was a good way to fortify my friendship with Billy, so I gathered tools, sticks, a can of tar, shingles, and off I went, climbing the ladder to the roof of the house.

"Luc, take a piece of stick over there, open the can of tar, and start filling up the spots where the shingles are lifted," the foreman said.

Great, I thought, *you don't have to be a rocket scientist to do that.*

As I toiled away at the work, talking to Billy, whistling, and complaining about the height and the cool wind, I was flooded with memories of my dad when, at age twelve, I was assigned the job of runner for him and my older brothers, who were doing exactly what I was doing in Windsor on our home in New Brunswick.

What's a runner? Normally, it's the less talented carpenter, a handyman with no particular talent who the foreman orders to get beer, lunch, bring up the tile, the tar, hammers, and so on. At twelve years of age, I was already a bit stressed out, since I wanted to impress the old man and my asshole big brothers.

At one point, Dad turned to me and said, "*Va chercher l'aiguine!*"

I had heard that term before, but for the life of me, I had no idea what the hell it meant. Too shy or too stupid to ask for an explanation, I climbed down the ladder, headed for the basement tool shed, and sat down.

"Okay, what the hell is an *aiguine*?" I asked myself. I looked around and tried to figure out which tool would be required in a roof repair operation run by "Ti-Route Ouellette," my old man. The lights don't come on, so I picked up an old measuring tape and proceeded to the roof.

It was probably ninety degrees outside at that time (Canada had not turned metric yet). My brothers and my dad were sweating from the heat while I was sweating from fear. I handed him the measuring tape, and he looked at me with his blue eyes.

"C'est pas un hostie d'aiguine ça, maudit niaiseu," he said in his Acadian French.

For the first time in my life, I was really embarrassed and angry. I took the tape measure, threw it on the roof, and asked him in my own charming language, "What the hell is an *aiguine?*"

"It's a saw, stupid," Dad said. "A saw."

"Okay, Dad," I said. "Thanks for the words of wisdom. Now I am politely declaring to you that you can take this job and shove it where the sun doesn't shine. I quit!"

That was the last time Ti-Route and his twelfth child worked on any kind of carpentry together. Why didn't he just say, "Go get the saw?" That incident bothered me until I was a grown man, but we laughed about it later. As I mentioned, he was an Acadian Brayon from northwestern NB, and I was raised in an Acadian French school, so the lingo was not the same. The heat had caused him to revert to his native lingo. I had no idea what he was talking about, and I was too hot and scared to ask for a clarification. I have learned many lessons since then, such as, if you don't understand something that someone you respect or are intimidated by says, make sure you ask for clarification.

Years later, I giggled thinking that there was a guy who, with my mom, put fifteen rotten kids on Earth. No wonder he lost his cool once in a while. I did not have that problem with my son, because after that incident with Dad, I decided that working the land and repairing houses, cars, tools, and so on was not for me. I would get educated and make money so that I could hire people to do those things. Today, my son knows more about chores around the house than I do.

The only time you would hear me talk about a runner again was in my job as a cop, only it had a new definition: a person who transported illegal drugs from point A to point B for the purpose of delivering to a drug trafficker or traffickers. I also realized I was better at catching runners than being one.

The roofing job took about an hour. With a few bucks in Billy's pocket, we headed off for the dump house. Billy asked me to stop at the beer store and returned with a couple of twelve packs. As we drove, the discussion went from women to drugs to money.

We arrived at the motel and, after entering, Billy pointed across the street to a new residential area. He told me that they had stolen many pieces of wood and other items from the construction site to sell for extra cash to get dope. He was comfortable, loud, and abrasive as usual, but I noted that Ken changed the subject every time we talked about Billy's criminal activities. I surmised that he was worried that Billy would admit to crimes in which Ken was involved.

I showed Billy the application forms I had obtained for two jobs in the city, one at St. Clair College and the other at Ambassador Cleaners. He gave me directions to those places and then added that he knew the owner of Ambassador Cleaners and that his name was Fred Kruger. I told him that I was headed out to deliver the application forms and would be back soon. Again, I hoped that they would discuss the Lougheed murder in my absence and that the conversation would be captured on the wire.

I left the room and met up with Viper, the IC of the cover team, at a local coffee shop. While I sat and drank coffee, Viper dispatched another officer named Chico to deliver the application form. Chico returned later and informed me that he had handed the form to Karen Kruger, the owner's wife, and that she had told him there was no one there by the name of Fred Kruger.

Good one, Billy, I thought. "Fred" was short for "Freddy Kruger" from the *Nightmare on Elm Street* movies. I thought it was funny.

I returned to the dump house and told Billy and Ken that I had delivered the application form to Mrs. Kruger and then said, "Good one, boys."

They laughed, and at that point, I realized that they both thought I wasn't too bright due to my sloppy roof work and my not knowing who Freddy Kruger was. That was fine with me. As they teased and harassed me, I thought that was exactly what friends did to each other, so I threw out a couple of expletives, and we all laughed.

At one point in the conversation, I introduced the story of my wife in New Brunswick. I mentioned that she had kicked me out of the house and that I would certainly like someone to put her out of her misery.

"Hey, Luc, that's the mother of your kids," Billy said, sounding serious. "You shouldn't say or even think of things like that."

I concluded that Billy had a bit of heart somewhere in his useless body. He had no problem killing another person, just as long as it wasn't the mother of his kid. The more I complained about my wife, the more he repeated that I shouldn't do her in and that nobody around Windsor would kill a mother anyway.

A short while later, we left the room, and I dropped off Ken and then Billy. He would talk to me about the murder eventually; I was now sure of it. It had been a good day!

7
THE DOWN HOME TRIP

During my many visits to Billy's house, I met several individuals, Billy's so-called friends. They were people of every age, both male and female, all stoned or drunk. It was not a very secure or sane environment. I concluded that it was a crack house where the neighborhood drug users would enter without knocking, grab a seat, and smoke, drink, sleep, curse, and all the other things that normal Canadians did. Yeah right!

Many of the conversations in the room included Lougheed's murder. I gathered that each and every person who visited knew who had killed him, but no one would rat on the culprit. All of the conversations included comments like, "That guy was an asshole; I'm glad they killed him."

It also became clear, however, that none of them knew the whole story, and if they did, they didn't

care or they were scared of big, bad Billy. So, on it
went, referring to Lougheed's death like it was a
TV show, but no names were ever mentioned in my
presence. It was frustrating, and I was worried that
the job could go on forever if we didn't come up with
some kind of plan to get Billy out of the house and
away from his friends.

The house was Billy's refuge from the world.
There, he had control. No one would snitch on
him. He felt secure there, and our task was to make
him feel less in control and not so secure. Then he
would do what we all do when we're uncomfortable: sit back and not talk or interact with anyone.
I knew Billy well enough to conclude that he might
be uncomfortable, but his personality was such that
he had to be in control. The fact that he treated me
right but thought I was a dummy from down east
convinced me that if we removed him from his comfortable surroundings for a few days, he might react
differently. He would feel vulnerable and be quiet or
else rant and rave in his normal way. I put my money
on the latter.

I discussed the situation with Neal and told
him that I didn't feel we were progressing. I said
we should come up with a plan to get Billy to leave
the house and join me with Ken for a set period of
time—but not too long, because I couldn't handle
the guy for any length of time. Neal agreed and said

he would think about it and see what could be done. Such thoughts crossed my mind on a daily basis, but for the life of me, I could not figure out a scenario to achieve that goal.

It's funny how often my mouth gets me in trouble. As we tried to figure out a way to get Billy out of the house, I informed Neal that I needed a break to rest, gather my thoughts, and re-energize. I told him that I would go back to New Brunswick to see my family and return in a couple of weeks in the hope of having more success in the operation.

"Yeah, you're right, bud, you need to take a break to see your family," Neal said. "Actually, it would probably be good for everyone. Take the unmarked to get home, and when you're ready, you can come back."

Wow, that was great! I got to take the car home. No airplane, no waiting, and a long drive home to relax, gather my thoughts, review my actions, and see where I could improve to get Billy.

"Great, thanks, Neal. I'll take you up on that," I said.

I would be away for a week, so I had to find a way to let Ken and Billy know that I would be going home for a reason other than rest. I was happy and excited that I would get to go home to see my family and get some much-needed R&R.

The following day, I advised Neal that I would be taking off on March 15 and be gone for a few days.

"I've been thinking about this," Neil replied. "You're headed home to see your family. Why don't you take Billy and Ken with you?"

I should have known! Neal's a good guy, but offering me the use of his unmarked unit for a nineteen-hour drive and then back was a pretty expensive favor, and I realized he had already thought it all out.

"You, Ken, and Billy can head to New Brunswick. Drop Ken and Billy at his sister's place in Grand Sault, and then you can continue to your home."

It was brilliant. We just had to come up with a story as to why I had to go home and then invite Ken to come along, telling him that I would only be for a few days, and then I would be coming right back. I was to make sure that Billy was present when I asked Ken to come along. He most certainly would inquire if he could come, too, especially considering it was only for a few days.

The story we came up with was that my wife was taking me to the cleaners and wanted a divorce. There was a court hearing on Friday morning, and I had to attend to ensure that her lawyer didn't take me for everything, especially custody of my kids. The boys would wire up the car and record our conversations. That way Billy would no longer be in his safe, cozy dump and, hopefully, he would talk about the murder.

I thought it was possible, but only after we settled a few concerns. For one, I would be alone in the vehicle for hours with a suspected murderer and an agent whom I did not trust. For all I knew, they might blow me away, drop my body along the 401, and just keep driving. I needed to find another UC to join us to watch my back. A lot of discussion took place, and then we contacted a friend of mine who was a UC with the Niagara Police Service to ask if he would join our adventure to New Brunswick.

The only remaining issue was that Billy had no money. There was no way he could afford to feed himself and pay for a motel room if we had to stop along the way, and there was no way I could be seen as the guy who financed everything for him and Ken. What could we do?

While we tried to solve that problem, we also worked on various scenarios to include another passenger in the car, one that Ken and Billy didn't know. Would they talk about the murder in front a new face? I wasn't convinced of that, and Ken echoed my concern when I told him about the plan.

"There is no way Billy's going to talk about killing Lougheed with a stranger in the car," he said. "We have a hard time enough time getting him to talk to you now."

It made sense. As much as I was worried about being alone with them in the car, I accepted the fact that bringing someone else along would not work.

As I mentioned, the Windsor police had an effective spin team, who I was sure would be close enough to rescue me if something went awry. A lot of discussion ensued about using them. Again, I had to make a decision and show that I had balls and could handle any situation should things get out of hand.

One problem with having the Windsor police spin team tail me was that they were a municipal police force, so they only had jurisdiction in Ontario. Who would cover me across Quebec and New Brunswick? I decided to call Gary Legresley, my former boss in the RCMP drug unit in Bathurst and an old friend. I explained the plan to him, and he was eager to help in any way he could.

"You can drop off your agent in Grand Sault and, to be alone with Billy, you can drive to Campbellton, where I'll have a couple of UCs take Billy off your hands and make sure he's under control while you go home and rest a bit."

He added that he would contact his counterpart in Ontario and set up a meeting so that the Mounties' spin team would pick me up at the Quebec/Ontario border and follow me all the way home. I thought that was great, but it was also getting complicated. The more people involved, the more problems we could encounter, and that was certainly not what I was looking for.

Nevertheless, following my discussion with Gary and meetings with Neal, things seemed to be going well. It was just a matter of everyone involved understanding that their primary job was to keep me safe and to make sure Billy felt comfortable believing he was leaving Windsor for a breather away from the scene of the crime. Then and only then might he open up and spill the beans—that is, if there were any beans to spill. I felt comfortable that it would work and that it was just a matter of time. Never for one minute did I doubt the professionalism of the Windsor boys, but I did not know the RCMP boys, and it was important to me that they saw me and were able to identify me before the journey began.

With that part of the plan in motion, we turned to our final problem: Billy had no money! How would he be able to afford motels and food? A lot of thought and discussion went into solving that problem. We could do some break and enters and sell the product for cash. We could do a thousand other things to get cash, but they were all criminal offences, and I did not want to be, nor could I be, involved in such illegal activities. It's not like the movies where the undercover cop is worse than the bad guys he's trying to get. We had to come up with another scam to get money for Billy, to have him believe it had been obtained illegally. By doing so, we would also strengthen my cover. I decided to let things play out and see what happened. There were all sorts of ideas, but it was another thing putting them into practice. Billy was a pretty resourceful guy, and I was confident that he would find the cash. First though, we had to ensure that he would be part of the travelling circus.

The following day, I informed Ken that we were going to visit Billy and that while there, we would discuss our women and the trouble we were having with them. Then I would announce that I was planning a trip to New Brunswick for a couple of days, because I had to see my lawyer prior to going to court with my old lady to see what I could salvage of my funds, and especially my kids. I would ask Ken if he was interested in coming along. I would tell him I could drop him off in Grand Sault with his sister on Thursday night and come back to pick him up on Saturday morning after my Friday meeting with the lawyers.

At Billy's, I made the request loud enough that Billy heard, and, as expected and hoped, he took the bait.

"What's that? You guys going to NB?"

After explaining the reason for my trip, he had that look in his eyes, like, "Please, take me." In the most nonchalant way, I told him he could jump in with us as long as he paid his way.

"I'll take care of the gas, but you're on your own for food and motels," I explained. "If you're okay with that, I'm leaving on Wednesday and planning to drive all night. My court appearance is Friday morning, and I'm coming back on Saturday morning. I'll pick you guys up, and away we go."

Billy was thrilled about going to New Brunswick. He had never been there. That didn't surprise me. I don't think he had ever left Windsor.

Our plan was taking shape, but I knew he had no money to afford a motel room and meals.

"Don't worry about that," Billy said. "I'll find the bucks."

Billy did not seem at all concerned about finding the money. As much as it was important for him to come with us, I could not figure out a way for money to fall into that asshole's hands so that I could be assured he would be onboard. With that crew, it was not unusual that they would be late or not show up at all for any reason. I half expected him to cancel at the last minute, stating that he could not find the money, but we would do everything in our power to make sure that didn't happen.

8
THE PURSE SCAM

I didn't think the trip would cost Billy more than a couple hundred bucks. I was paying the gas, so all he had to worry about was his food and a motel room, if needed. It became evident quickly that Billy already had an idea in mind.

At about two in the afternoon, after briefing with Neal and the boys, I picked up Ken at his apartment. The investigators had told me that he did not want to leave Windsor and go to New Brunswick. He had not mentioned that to me. I figured he was leery for two reasons. One, he wasn't comfortable with me any longer, and two, he was worried about bringing Billy to his sister's house in Grand Sault. I could not blame him. Billy was a loud, obnoxious individual who would certainly be noticed in small town Grand Sault. His sister was a quiet, law-abiding citizen who worried a lot about her big brother in Ontario. She knew he had a dope problem and was not impressed by it but could not convince him to seek help and stop his trafficking. But he was her brother, and she loved him.

Billy was a whole other story. If he started drinking or snorting down there, the entire town would hear about it. I think that's what bothered Ken more. He could not be sure that Billy would act like a human, but he was comforted that he would only be there for a couple of days.

After we gave the secret knock at Billy's place, Trashcan opened the door and directed us to the living room, where Billy was sitting with a few other guys watching TV. We had a short chat, during which I told Billy that I had received a few parking tickets where I parked near his place. Billy stated that since the cops had seen my car at his place earlier, I could expect to be harassed even more. That sounded good to me, because it helped solidify my cover story. We stayed for about thirty minutes and then decided to leave.

Billy followed us to the kitchen and informed me that he had a little thing to do to get some money to go with us. When I asked, he told me that there was a little leather shop not far from his place where they had cowboy boots, leather jackets, and other leather goods. After ripping them off, he would sell boots and jackets to raise funds.

Josh Ouellette

"How you gonna do that, Billy?" I asked.

"Smash and grab, man, smash and grab! We're gonna go take a look at the joint and see what's the best way to do this."

I wasn't too sure about the smash and grab thing, and I certainly knew that I could not smash anything or break in anywhere for Billy to get money to go to NB. But off we went to check out the leather shop. We were to look for any security cameras, bars on the windows, the location of back door, and so on. If it was all good, we'd go back later at night to smash the window and grab some leather goods for resale.

When we entered the cowboy shop, a huge man with long hair and a beard was sitting behind the counter. He eyed us closely. In the five minutes I was inside, I noted bars on every window and at least three surveillance cameras—one on the front door that caught people entering, one behind the big guy at the counter, and another on the inside of the front door catching people leaving the store. If there were so many cameras, he had probably been hit before and was protecting his property thoroughly. Smash and grab was out. Too many bars. So was break and enter at night because of at least three cameras inside and outside of the shop.

After a few minutes of browsing, I left the shop and waited for my passengers in the parking lot. Once in the car, Billy seemed a little less confident about his smash and grab caper. I told him it was a waste of time. With all those cameras, there was probably an alarm as well, silent or noisy, that would either scare the hell out of us or cause our police friends to descend on us like the cavalry.

"I'm not doing this, Billy, it's not smart. We'll be caught in ten minutes, and there goes my trip to New Brunswick. I'll miss the meeting with my lawyers and probably lose custody of my kids."

"Well, shit man, I got no money," he said.

"We'll find some, Billy, don't worry," I assured him. "You're not going to miss your first visit to NB. We'll figure out a way." There had to be a way to find cash without having to give it to him outright.

Billy asked me to drop him off at Wahoo's place, which I did, and then I dropped off Ken at his apartment. I figured Billy was stopping at Wahoo's place to borrow money but could not be sure. We simply had to figure out a way to get the bucks.

I returned to the dump house and met with Neal, Brags, and the boys. Detectives Cliff Lovell and Dave "Perp" Perpich briefed me on an exercise they had planned out that we hoped would suffice to ensure Billy had enough money to go with me.

"We've planted a car with Michigan plates in the lot next to the Becker's Convenience store close to the dump house," they explained. "The doors are unlocked, and on the back seat will be a lady's purse that contains a couple of hundred dollars in Canadian and American currency along with a fake driver's license and other documents. Once Billy and Ken are in the car and you're on your way to the dump house, tell the boys you need to stop at the convenience store to pick up smokes. Go into the store, buy a pack of smokes, and when you come out, look over into the car, open the door, and grab the purse. Throw it in the back seat and get the hell out of there."

I thought it was a great idea, and I knew it would work as planned. Things were running smoothly. I know I've said this before, but these Windsor cops impressed the hell out of me. I had been at that convenience store many times, even with Billy and Ken, so there would be no worries and nothing out of the ordinary if I stopped there to pick up smokes.

At about 0900 hours on March 18, I attended a briefing with all of the teams involved in the operation: the Windsor investigators, the Windsor spin team, and the RCMP spin team. The purpose of the meeting was to make sure everyone was on track with what would happen on the trip to New Brunswick. It also made me feel more comfortable that the Mounties would be able to identify me easily should there be any problems on the way. The plan for the day was to pick up Ken and Billy, proceed to the convenience store, and, hopefully, after a successful purse scam, continue to the dump house, change, and head off to New Brunswick. If only it could be that simple!!

I took off and picked up Ken at his apartment. Then we continued to Billy's house, where, after knocking a few times, he opened the door in his underwear, all shriveled up and a bit hyper.

"Are you set? Let's go, man," I said.

Billy got dressed, grabbed an extra T-shirt and a pair of underwear, put on his jacket, and we were ready to go.

Billy asked if he could drop off a package at his daughter's place. I agreed, but I also said I had to stop at the convenience store and then go to my room to pick up my luggage. So far, so good.

We dropped off some clothing to Billy's daughter and then proceeded to the convenience store. Upon arriving, I noted that the Michigan-plated car, which had the purse, was parked facing the curb, and another car was parked to its right, making it impossible for me to step out of the driver's side and glance nonchalantly into the vehicle to see the purse. Shit! I needed to be close enough to the car to make it look natural, but that meant I had to go to the rear of my car on my passenger's side and, by luck, notice the purse. It was pretty tricky, but I had no choice.

I got out of the vehicle, walked into the store, stayed inside for two or three minutes, and then returned. I walked to the passenger side, kicked the tires, and happened to glance into the Michigan vehicle. It must have seemed a little weird, but it had to be done. Then I turned to the boys and pointed inside the car. I checked the door, found it unlocked, removed the purse and threw in the back seat of my car onto Billy's lap. It was an awfully awkward move, but when I jumped into the driver's seat, there was no mention of it except for a couple of comments like, "Let's get the fuck outta here."

We left the parking lot quickly but without attracting attention and proceeded to the dump house. Billy had already opened the purse and found some cash, and I told him to put it back until we got to my place. I could see that he was happy, and I knew I was, since we had managed to get some money to finance his share of the trip and I had re-enforced my cover once again.

We entered the room, and I proceeded to the washroom to pick up my stuff for the trip. Meanwhile, they celebrated and congratulated me on my luck. Billy counted the cash, and there was approximately $270. He started splitting it up, and I made the mistake of telling him to keep my share; I didn't need it. I guess I was a bit excited. Giving them my share of the money was something I should not have done. Again, it was the down homer in me. A bad guy, especially an undercover bad guy, rarely gave things away, especially money that he had obtained himself. I guess Billy didn't see the gesture to be out of the ordinary, and I blew it off as another dangerous mistake that I could not afford to make again.

Billy gave Ken half the cash and then, after checking the rest of the purse, told me that we had to find a mailbox on the way out of the town. When I asked why, he explained that he had no problem taking the woman's money but that it was hell trying to replace a driver's license and credit cards. Again, in his twisted state of mind, Billy showed a little bit of compassion for a stranger who had just been the victim of theft.

"We'll drop it in the first mailbox we find, and at least she won't have to do all the running around to replace the papers," he said.

Billy never ceased to amaze me. I believed he had committed the cold-blooded murder of Ron Lougheed, another human being, without any sign of remorse, but then he turned around and did not want to cause grief to another person after being involved in the theft of her wallet. I thought about that for quite a while, and, as a matter of fact, I still do to this day. I concluded that people, whether rich or poor, educated or uneducated, stupid or smart, have a good streak in them, or maybe it is better described as a soft spot.

I remembered an earlier conversation with Billy about my problems with my fictitious wife, who was taking me to the cleaners by asking for a divorce and taking my kids. I insinuated that I should have her killed and be rid of the problem.

"No, man, you can't do that. She's the mother of your children. I couldn't do it," he had replied. At the time, I thought it weird that a guy who went around trying to act tough and intimidate everyone did not have the intestinal fortitude to whack my pain-in-the-ass wife. There were only two possible answers to that inconsistency: he did not kill innocent people for his friends or he only killed people who had done him wrong. I concluded that he would only kill my fictitious wife if she did him wrong, and, obviously, that would never happen. So, he was not a contract killer! I was beginning to get to know Billy. He was a rowdy, uneducated, and boisterous bully only to people he knew and only to those who showed fear when he started his rants. I felt better. Billy would only kill me if I became a danger to him, and so far, I was not.

We were still sniffing each other out like wolves in our beautiful North. He was not your regular guy though. He appeared to be open and comfortable with me; I believed that strongly. He didn't think I was a cop, because if he did, he would have found an excuse to get away from me. He wasn't smart enough to play games with the cops, because they scared him. They were the alpha males in this town, and he feared them. I suppose if he ever had a serious encounter with Neal, Brags, Lovell, or Perpich, which I'm positive he did during the course of the homicide investigation, his bullying personality would have become what is known in police circles as "a pussy." I giggled to myself when I thought of Billy sitting and talking with Neal. I pictured Neal with his glaring eyes, deep, controlled voice, and his index finger in Billy's face giving Billy a lecture on how to become a human being and meek, little Billy boy with his head and eyes down, totally fear stricken. That would have been worth the money.

I also realized that Billy really wanted to take a break from Windsor. I believed he was having some kind of remorse and was regretting his lifestyle. He had a daughter whom he loved, apparently, and brothers who visited him regularly. So he was not that far from being a good person. Perhaps he regretted his choices. Maybe after killing Lougheed he was accepting the fact that his past life was useless and that the remainder of it would not be any better. He needed to get out of his environment to try and regain the freedom and peace of mind that he had prior to all the heat coming down from his actions the previous year. Just like anyone, he wanted to feel safe. He wanted to be with people he knew and trusted, and he wanted to be able to regain that security blanket that he probably had in his younger years. He must have believed he had the possibility of feeling that way again with Ken and I on a road trip to spend a couple of days with the nice, down home people of Grand Sault, NB.

Billy knew Ken, and he trusted him at least fifty percent of the time. He also wanted to trust me but did not know enough about me yet. So far, my appearance, my actions, and my demeanor had sufficed to support my cover, and it was fundamental that I maintained my quiet, sit-in-the-corner-and-only-speak-to-when-asked attitude. I was reading him well and knew that by the time I got to New Brunswick, Billy would tell me the *who, what, when, where,* and *why* of Ron Lougheed's demise.

I had learned early in my career that I could not underestimate anyone. I could not conclude anything until all of the information was clear and precise and I was satisfied "beyond a reasonable doubt" that the information I had obtained was above reproach. I believed strongly that the truth would never be challenged for any length of time. The defense lawyers would attempt to muddy the facts. They would try to confuse the witness and, if they succeeded, their criminal client might walk. I was unimpressed with the lawyers' tactics, but I couldn't get confused if I was telling the truth!

With this case, as in many others, I was dealing with individuals who lacked morals, self-respect, and respect for others. Most people I met, good or bad, in my long career, could tell if another person was telling the truth or lying. I could. I was trained to watch the eyes, the speech, the body language, and so on, and I could make a pretty sound judgement call about a person. As a police investigator, I could not have tunnel vision. I had to consider all of the evidence. I had to be diligent and proceed in a calculated and open-minded manner. If Billy had murdered Lougheed, I would do everything in my power to help Neal and the Windsor boys prosecute him to the full force of the law, as they had done many times before and no doubt continue to do. Such professionalism and hard work for me as a cop in Canada, whether from New Brunswick or Ontario, was understood and expected. Every citizen of my country is protected by its police to the best of their ability. They leave no stone unturned. If someone commits a crime, the Canadian police forces will go to great lengths to apprehend the person and ensure he or she faces up to his or her responsibilities.

I was reminded of how great my country is when, on one of my evenings off, Neal invited the boys and me to a promotion party across the river with the Detroit homicide unit, where one of Neal's friends was celebrating twenty years as a Detroit police officer. It was a nice surprise. I also wondered aloud why he was being celebrated after only twenty years of service. Where I was from, celebrations were held after an officer did twenty-five and then thirty years. Neal told me that Detroit was not like Canada. It was rare to see a Detroit cop make it to twenty years. They either quit, got turfed, or were killed before then. So, everyone was celebrating this honest cop's twenty years of service, and we, the boys from across the river, were invited.

I was a little bit intimidated by that crew. I'll never forget walking up the steps of the side of a building into a large, open bar with several patrons enjoying a cold one. Even weirder for this Canuck was the fact that a lot of them were wearing a sidearm on their belt or around their shoulder and holding an alcoholic beverage in one hand and a smoke in the other. I wondered what would happen if one of them got pissed off at another and decided to deal with the situation in the cowboy fashion. One of the boys told me that the joint was all police and that there was no shop talk. Sure, I thought, what else would a bunch of cops in a bar talk about?

In Canada, police did the same thing as their American counterparts, except that no weapons were visible or allowed. We talked about other things, but we certainly talked shop. Many an argument had broken out, and many were solved by a visit to the back of the building where, as in sports, women, and the weather, the strongest survived.

The bar was filled with friendly faces who came to introduce themselves. Most were Detroit cops, but some were from the FBI and other law enforcement agencies. Once word got around that I was from New Brunswick, a few of the boys came over to say hello. I approached the honored guest. After I congratulated him and wished him the best, he informed me that he had been to New Brunswick on a holiday once and really liked the place.

"I really don't understand you Canadian cops," he said. "They brought you here all the way from the coast to infiltrate a group of losers who are suspected of killing one of their own buddy losers. It must be costing a fortune for both departments to have you here. Here, once we get the call that one of these guys got killed, we have a very limited amount of time to solve the crime. We're overwhelmed with an average of three homicides a day, so if there aren't any leads, the case quickly becomes a cold case."

He paused before continuing. "Actually, a boy like the one you were brought here for would probably not even get us excited. They're involved in the game, and they know that this could happen to them. Why should the taxpayers of Detroit pay to investigate the demise of a useless human being?"

I thought it was kind of harsh, but I also under-stood how easily it could happen not only in America but also in Canada. At the time I worked in Windsor, eight homicides had taken place that year. During that same time period, Detroit had over six hundred. As my new friend had said, the city of Detroit alone averaged three homicides a day. That information blew my mind and made me glad that I was a Canadian down homer. I had lots to think and worry about, but I felt good. Billy had money, the car was wired up, and soon we would be on our way to New Brunswick. I would have ample time to talk with Billy and, hopefully, get the information we needed.

After I grabbed my luggage and finished up some last-minute stuff, we were off. I was aware that the spin team was all around us, that they would follow us to the Ontario/Quebec border, where the RCMP spin team would take over for the remainder of the trip. I was aware that all conversations in the vehicle would be recorded by a wire setup in the vehicle and that I was covered by my fake cell phone when not in the car. I would call in once in a while if I thought I needed to, and my protectors on the spin team would pass information onto me when I stopped for gas or food. It was a pretty good plan. "Don't panic," I told myself. "Be cool. All will go well."

Ken and Billy were raring to go, especially now that Billy had some money and would not be bumming from us. I hadn't thought much about the nineteen-hour drive through Ontario and Quebec, but I told myself I would play it by ear. I did not want one of my passengers offering to drive if I looked too tired, so it was important for me to focus and stay awake. I was determined never to be alone with them. If they planned to do me in, it would have to be while I was driving at highway speed, and that, I was convinced, was not the way they wanted to leave this planet.

Prior to take off, Ken loaded the car with my empty beer containers, which the Windsor boys had placed in my room. There was a lot of them, and the cash could come in handy on the road. Billy decided to take a shower as I loaded the car with luggage. Finally, we were off!

First things first: I had to fill up the gas tank and get some smokes, and Billy and Ken wanted to stop at the beer store to pick up some refreshments for on the way to the east coast. Then we made our way to the 401.

9

IN THE CAR WITH A KILLER

Call it the jitters, excitement, or worry, but I had not seen any of my compatriots from the spin team since I entered the dump house. Of course, I was not supposed to see them, because if I had seen them, maybe my two buddies would have seen them, too. I had complete faith in those guys, and I knew they were there, but I was still a little nervous, especially since I had no means of contacting them. They, on the other hand, had been well briefed and had the necessary information on the target, the agent, and me, including a description of the vehicle, what we were wearing, and our destination. They were also in direct contact with the Windsor police investigators, and a member was monitoring our conversation on a twenty-four-hour basis—or so I hoped!

An operation of that magnitude had a high level of security. Information was divulged only to those who needed to know. Both spin teams were aware of the case, as were the Windsor police investigators, but that was it. We did not get on the phone and call all of the police forces along the Trans-Canada advising them that a cop, an agent, and a target in a homicide case were rolling down the 401 through their jurisdiction. First, it was dangerous for too many people to know, since there was a chance that a cop or his girlfriend or wife would let it leak. It was exciting for anyone and, of course, human nature pushed people to be more curious and ask too many questions. Sometimes it was just nice for someone to boast about some important information he or she had to which not everyone was privy.

That was my problem. I got so involved I tended to exaggerate things, such as saying the beaches in New Brunswick had the warmest waters north of South Carolina. Some Ontario people who had been to New Brunswick knew better, but the everyday mortal assumed it was fact. Believe me, folks, I'm not exaggerating when I say that is an exaggeration. It's cold as hell there even in June and July. I don't know where that statement came from, but the tourism board of my province had advertised the phenomena, and even I, as a New Brunswicker, could not understand why. It might have brought first-time tourists to NB to spend their hard-earned holiday cash one time, but once they realized they had been deceived, they would never return. Worse, they would go home and tell their family and friends that New Brunswickers were either full of it or hot blooded, and then no one would come to visit New Brunswick's beaches. All that to say, the fewer people who knew about the operation, the safer it was for me.

As we drove, the boys cracked a beer, and the chatter was mainly about New Brunswick lobster, Ken's girlfriend problems, and the weather. When we rode past the Chatham, Ontario exit sign, Ken mentioned that he had lived there for a while before heading further west to Windsor.

"Yeah, this is where we wanted to bring the body, but we didn't have enough gas," Billy said out of the blue.

"Really? So where did you dump it?" I inquired.

"On the west side," he answered.

Billy's statement caught me by surprise, but I thought that any more questions would cause him to distrust me. It was a long ride, and he still felt in control. He recognized some of the places we passed and felt at home. More inquiries would only serve to pressure him, and there was a risk he would shut me out. That would change soon enough. There was ample time for Billy and I to open up and become true brothers when I told him about my problems with my fictitious wife and he told about Lougheed's death. Not knowing what Billy meant by the "west side," I considered it to be another bit of information that the investigators could use in the event I was unable to get an admission from Billy. Upon our return, admission or not, they would certainly have another meeting with their suspect, and that little tidbit of info would be used during the interview process. It was a fundamental procedure that the police investigators would follow. By mentioning it, Billy would help the officers put the pieces of the puzzle together. If he told me about the west side, I was certain he had told other people from his crew, and that would add to the pressure on Billy and would certainly help a judge or a jury decide on his guilt. That was for another time though. For the moment, we carried on down the 401 and talked about many things.

In the midst of one of those conversations, I saw lights in my rearview mirror. It was an OPP officer. I had been flagged for speeding.

Great! I thought. *What do I say now?* I hoped he didn't check the identity of my passengers, because then I would probably get a much larger ticket than I would have if I were with my wife and family. It was not a good time for me to flash my badge or tell him, "I'm sorry, brother, I'm a NB cop on an undercover job. Please don't give me a ticket."

After telling my friends not to say a word, I rolled down my window and observed the officer approach through my side view mirror.

"Good afternoon, sir," he said. "I'm stopping you because you were going one hundred and thirty-one in a one hundred zone. Can I see your driver's license and registration, please?"

"Sure, officer," I replied as I handed over my paperwork. He glanced at my passengers and then returned to his vehicle. I saw him raise his radio microphone to his mouth.

Nothing to worry about, I told myself. *He's just making sure all my papers are correct, because he probably wants to give me more fines.*

As usual, I was a little stressed out about being stopped by a cop, even though I was a cop. They made me nervous, and they were always bearers of bad and expensive news.

A few minutes later, he returned and handed me a ticket. "Slow down, sir," he said politely. Then he returned to his vehicle.

I started driving away with him about fifty feet behind me until he pulled over onto a side road and disappeared.

Shit, man, I gotta watch my speed or I'll never make it home, I reminded myself. I don't remember the amount of the fine, but I was confident that Neal would call the young officer's boss and explain the situation, thus removing my alias from Ontario's list of traffic offenders.

We were making good time as we passed through Toronto. Billy was still talking about cops when he looked to his right and noted a large tractor trailer. It was hauling a trailer full of pigs. Billy laughed.

"Look man, the pigs, they're following us, they're all over the place, those bastards."

We all laughed, even when my asshole agent buddy replied, "You're right, man. They're probably a lot closer than you think."

I felt my blood pressure rise and made a note to myself that I would kick Ken's ass for his stupid comment once all of this was over.

The next time Billy brought up the murder was near Brockville when we were talking about guns. "That's what I should have done," Billy said. "I should have done him with a hammer. Yeah, I should have done him with a hammer."

He didn't elaborate, but I understood that it would have been a lot easier for him to get rid of a hammer that had no description or registered owner, unlike a gun, which could be traced to an owner and, after more research, required an explanation on how it ended in Billy's hands. He was clearly worried about it. As I mentioned earlier, I was not aware of the small amount of evidence the cops had gathered. I did not even know what type of gun had been used except for what I had heard in conversations or while listening to comments made at Billy's place. As I drove, I became increasingly confident that Billy had committed the homicide or, at the very least, had been there when Lougheed was killed. However, I did not want to put all of my eggs in one basket and conclude that he had done it and that Wahoo was not involved.

I also realized that since my arrival in Windsor, I had met Wahoo only once. I also noted that Billy had visited Wahoo at his house only once and spoken to him just one time over the phone while I was there. Why? Perhaps both parties had been involved in a serious incident and neither wanted to go to jail. Therefore, they had decided that spending some time apart might make things easier. It would be like two kids doing something wrong and one party believing that his friend had overdone it. Was that what was going on between Billy and Wahoo? I wasn't sure. Billy did not seem concerned and kept telling me that Wahoo was his "brother" and that he would do anything for him.

The more I talked to Billy, and the more I observed him interact with his crew, the more I became convinced that Billy was responsible. He considered Wahoo a good friend and probably felt guilty for having disappointed him. Was Wahoo upset with him? Maybe Wahoo had decided that

Billy was nuts and did not want to be accused of the murder, so he was distancing himself from his long-time friend. I also thought Billy felt bad for putting Wahoo in the middle of the mess. Both men were probably hoping the police would go away. After all, if the police had sufficient evidence, why hadn't they arrested them? Billy and Wahoo probably thought that if they stayed out of trouble—and away from each other—the event would go away. The cops would get bored and move on to other crimes. It was a normal reaction to a situation that they both wished had not happened, and Billy and Wahoo were dealing with it in the best way they knew how. It was the common modus operandi of any human being who had done something wrong to distance him or herself from the event. That did not excuse the person, but it went a long way toward satisfying the person's need for self-preservation.

I believed our two suspects were human beings, but I also believed that one of them had a con-science, and the other did not, which was probably why Billy was in the car with me while Wahoo was safe at home. Billy was his own worst enemy. He was abrasive, loud, and ignorant, the type of person for which it was difficult to have any empathy. By that time, I had worked on close to one hundred under-cover operations, from drug trafficking to arson to other homicides, and I can say with sincerity that all of those drug traffickers and murderers displayed a bit of remorse for their crimes. I doubted that Billy would ever feel remorse. I was not a shrink, but I had been around long enough to know that the murder would not be the last of Billy's ventures in the crime world. Truth be told, Billy was just a poor, ignorant individual who wanted to survive the best he could. I was not aware of his upbringing, in what circumstances his parents raised him, or in what environment he had come of age, but that is no excuse. I believed him to be one of those individuals who always tried to take the easy way out. He would rather steal and whine to the Salvation Army for food and clothing than work for his money. I could not believe that a person living in Windsor did not have choices for work and living expenses. I tried with all my might to feel sorry for him, but for the life of me, I could not be sympathetic to him and his choices in life. Then again, if it weren't for people like Billy, there would be no need for cops, which would put people like me out of work.

So be it, I thought. *You're a bad guy. The majority of us are good people, so we must do everything in our power to protect people from people like you.*

We made several stops along the 401 for us to visit the little boys' room, to gas up, and to get some food before continuing on our stressful but merry way.

Between Kingston and Montreal, in a loud and excited conversation, Ken, in the back seat, badgered Billy about who all was involved in the homicide and specifically who and why they had used Ken's car to transport and dump the body. Ken ranted and complained for a while and then, out of the blue, Billy turned to me.

"Are you a cop?"

The question caught me off guard, but I stuttered and answered with my big toothless grin, unshaven face, and bald head. "Do I look like a cop, to you, Billy? It's none of my business, and I'm not interested in knowing anything. Don't worry about me, I'm cool!"

Time seemed to slow. I hoped that the goddam recorder was working. I figured that bit of conversation would make or break the case, and it was vital that I remembered every detail that he relayed to me just in case there was a problem with the recording equipment. I took several deep breaths, knowing that the mind and the memory often played tricks on people when they were in stressful situations. I calmed myself and concentrated on what he was saying. My recall of his admission would be of paramount importance in court later on, and I knew the recording would either back up my testimony or create more confusion.

You're a pro, man, calm down, relax and get your brain in recording mode for what is about to come.

I felt bad for the judge or the jury who would have to listen to our conversation. Every sentence was laced with curses and foul language. I tried to refrain, but I had to be one of them, so the conversation was a bit crazy.

"This stays in the car," Billy said. Then he informed us about the events in his house on the night of the murder. "He stole from me, right in my own house. He stole a smoke from my pack, which I had laid on the table between Wahoo and me."

Billy explained that he and Wahoo were at the kitchen table smoking crack and that Lougheed was upset that they did not offer him any. He became upset with them and said he would rat on them for past crimes.

"When he said that," Billy said, "I got up, walked to my bedroom, took out the twenty-two from my closet, walked back to him at the table, and shot him in the back of the head. He fell to the floor, then both Wahoo and I got up, kicked him a couple times in the head, and left him lying there for three hours. Later, we dragged him and threw him down the stairs to my basement."

Billy repeated the same thing at least three times to Ken. "I tell ya, Ken, straight up, I shot the fuck, because he was gonna rat on us."

I felt that Billy was reaching for some kind of support from us, and for the first time, I heard a cry for help in his voice. He was cleansing his soul. His and Wahoo's secret was finally out, and I gathered that he was relieved to have told someone else of his exploits. He was not proud of himself for killing Lougheed, but in his mind, he had no choice, since Lougheed would have snitched on them.

Here we go, I thought. Billy was complaining about how his feelings were hurt when Lougheed said that he would tell. It was a normal reaction for anyone—blame someone else for his wrongdoing, but to the point of putting a bullet in Lougheed's head? That was way too far. It was hard for me to sympathize with Billy. I thought of Lougheed and especially his family. He might have been a druggie, but did he deserve to be executed in cold blood? He was someone's son, brother, boyfriend. No one should have been put down in that fashion.

Billy continued his "confession," explaining that he had shot Lougheed with a sawed-off .22 caliber rifle and that he had bought the bullets himself. He said that .22 caliber bullets were the best, because when the bullet hit the skull, it broke up, and the cops couldn't do comparisons or any other form of ballistics analysis.

"Did you ever kill anyone, Ken?" Billy asked in a proud and authoritative way. "This is the first time

I shot someone in the side of the head. Normally I would look him straight in the eye, like the four others I killed, and wait until they begged for their lives."

In the same conversation, Billy informed us that the police had come to visit him and mentioned that the forensic lab had found traces of semen in Lougheed's anus. "That's impossible," Billy said. "When I shot him, he had just taken a shit, so there's no way they found semen."

I realized that the police had used the tactic to get him to admit to the killing. Most murderers didn't mind being called a "murderer," but there was no way they wanted to be referred to as a homosexual. Billy didn't fall for it though, and the investigation continued. So did his confession. He repeated several times that he had shot Lougheed, because Lougheed was going to rat on them.

Ken piped in and asked why, if Billy did it, did Wahoo tell him that he had done it. Billy went into great detail in his reply, talking to us like we were dummies.

"According to the Canada Evidence Act, the cops had to have the evidence or an admission from the actual person who committed the crime. In other words, if Wahoo is a suspect, then I can't be. That's why there's a rumor out there that I did it and another rumor that Wahoo did it."

Pretty smart, I thought. Billy believed, and probably rightfully so, that he wouldn't be charged unless the cops found specific evidence linking him to the shooting. Therefore, if he and Wahoo stuck to their story, the cops would never be able to charge him. The police had not located the weapon. When and if it was found, it could be tracked back to its original manufacturer, retailer, and original owner. More in-depth investigation would determine the final person who owned it, thus providing the information as to who pulled the trigger. The point remained that the weapon had not been found and probably only Billy and Wahoo knew where it was. It was part of my job to determine the location of the murder weapon. All in good time, my friend!

Billy's mood changed, and he became quiet and pensive and somewhat angry. He turned back to look at Ken. "Why did you and Minnie take the car to that fat ass at the salvage yard? He's the one that ratted us out to the cops. If you had just dumped the wheels, the cops wouldn't even have been notified, and they would not have begun an investigation that led to you, the owner, and then to us after you told him the car had been parked at my place."

The story brought some clarity to the sequence of events that had brought the police into Billy's life. Following the shooting in Billy's house, and after sobering up, Billy and his friends realized they had to dump the body somewhere to take suspicion away from his place and its inhabitants. It was unclear who was tasked to dump the body in the park, but I believe Billy and Wahoo did it. They used Ken's vehicle, which was parked in the yard, simply because they had no other means of transport, and probably because they were still stoned and not thinking clearly. They dumped the body in a Windsor park and then brought the vehicle back to Billy's house, where they also decided they should get rid of the car.

Ken and another cohort named Minnie took the vehicle to the savage yard to sell it but did not expect the owner to find the blood and call the cops. When that happened, Ken was arrested and taken into custody. After denying any involvement in the incident, he explained that he had left his car at Billy's place and that he had nothing to do with any murder. The police deduced that the crime had been committed in Billy's house, so they obtained a search warrant to look for any evidence that a homicide had occurred in there. Once the warrant was executed, the police found enough evidence to arrest and question Billy and Wahoo. That was where the challenge started for law enforcement. Lougheed's blood was found in the house—on the walls, the ceiling, and on the steps leading to the basement—as was lead, possibly from a small-caliber rifle. The interrogation of the suspects continued, to no avail. That was when the officers convinced Ken that if he helped them out, things would go easier for him. I was not made aware of any of that information upon my arrival in Windsor, so it helped me answer some questions.

During Billy's admission and Ken's rant, I kept reminding myself that I was damn lucky that it was dark in the vehicle. Billy could not see my dilated pupils, my red face from my high blood pressure, or my sweaty palms. Amen, finally, we had something! I felt relieved and happy inside, but I was anxious about the outcome of our adventure. I hoped the wire was working and that they had gotten the conversation on tape so that it could back up what I had heard.

Later, while briefing and being briefed by the RCMP spin team leader, he told me that, at one point between Kingston and Montreal, they were following me at speeds exceeding one hundred and sixty kilometers an hour. I couldn't believe it. That was when Billy was admitting his crime. And me, the big tough guy, I thought I was cool and under control. As I said earlier, the mind and the body react strangely when stressed out. I realized I wasn't such a tough guy after all! There were probably still a thousand unanswered questions to come from Neal and the troops, but I felt confident the case was taking a

Josh Ouellette

turn for the best and that they would have enough evidence to prosecute Billy.

Both of my friends drifted in and out of sleep. I used that time to gather my thoughts and ensure that all the details required for a successful prosecution would be in place. I pondered my good fortune. I had not planned on asking any direct questions about Billy's involvement in the murder. I was confident that we would talk and that he would, after trusting me, try to impress me with his ability to commit a murder and not get caught. Ken was the one who got him going, because he was angry that they had used his vehicle and especially that Wahoo had told him he did it. Basically, they trusted him enough to use his car to dump the body, but not enough to tell him exactly what had happened. By Ken ranting on, Billy felt compelled, in the confines of the car and with me present to clear the air and tell Ken exactly what had happened. I did not ask any more questions, but I knew that more information would become available as we went on. Billy had opened up, and now I was part of the circle of close friends who knew about the murder and who had done it. Eventually, he would come to realize that his big mouth had gone too far again. He would realize that two more guys knew the whole story, that he had killed Lougheed. What would he do? Panic or be cool and trust that we wouldn't give him up to the cops?

Billy had a lot on his mind, but I was convinced that he did not have any remorse. It was more like self-preservation. Also, as a typical human, he appreciated the limelight and he could not help but try to control the attention that the event brought into his life. The more I thought about it, the more I realized he was a lot like me. He wanted attention and respect. Some of us seek recognition by accomplishing something good, like putting bad guys away in jail. Others do it by committing crimes that put them in jail!

Okay, what was next? We had the who (Billy), the what (Lougheed's death), the when (that night at Billy's), the where (Billy's house), and the why (because Lougheed stole Billy's smokes and threatened to rat them out). All that was left for the investigators was to put it all together in a large, tidy package and hand it over to the Iceman with a recommendation of what charges should be laid. Once the crown attorney approved the charges, they would be laid in court, and the prosecution would begin. We were still quite a ways from that point, sitting in a car in Montreal and not having completed the trip, but I felt better. It was just a matter of taking this boy to New Brunswick and back, at which point Billy would be arrested and I could return home to my loved ones.

My two passengers came out of their slumber, and the conversation continued about anything and everything. Billy became philosophical and mentioned that, on his return from New Brunswick, he might move out west somewhere to get away from Windsor and all his problems. Ken, on the other hand, said it was too far for him. He would probably return to Grand Sault.

Billy returned to his original admission that he had killed many times for hire but that he had killed Lougheed because he was going to rat on him. I felt like Billy was boasting or that, in his minion mind, he figured that if he told me that he was a cold-blooded killer, I would be afraid to talk about what he had told me about the Lougheed killing. He emphasized the word "rat" and insinuated that he would have no problem dealing with me if I ever thought of saying anything.

"Don't worry, Billy," I said. "I'm cool. And besides, I don't care."

At the time, the thought of throwing him out of my moving car came to mind, but I decided it was unwise to kill the suspect. Besides, it would be difficult to explain to my fellow officers how a grown man had fallen out of a vehicle going at high speed on the highway near Montreal. Such is life.

I kept reminding myself that I was a good guy and that soon Billy would be the guest of her majesty's penitentiary system, so there was no need for me to dispose of this animal. I had to watch myself. I was starting to think and sound like those guys. It was probably time for rest and relaxation with normal human beings again. It became apparent to me why CISO insisted that we kept in contact with a shrink who could help us make sense of people like Billy and his nonsense. So many times, I had heard in my police career that there was a fine line between being a good cop and being a bad cop. I knew I was not a bad cop, that I was a law-abiding citizen, husband, and father who loved his good life.

I wondered often what it would be like to live the lives of different criminals. Would I be like Billy and his crew or like Michael Corleone in *The Godfather* ? My undercover duties helped clarify that for me. As a UC, I could have easily tasted the good life— parties, lots of dough, wine, women, and song. Or maybe I could have tasted a life like Billy's—in the twilight zone, stoned, drunk, and forever scamming for my next hit or my next meal. No thanks. I'd stick to my life as it was. That life had shown me that every choice I had made so far was pretty good. I went to bed at night knowing I had done well or that I had stopped some fool from committing more crimes. I liked that feeling, and I was sure most people would enjoy it, but not everyone could do it. I considered myself lucky to be one of those who could live the good life and then shave my head, take my teeth out, and become someone like Billy or Michael Corleone. I preferred Michael.

When we reached AutoRoute 20 near Quebec City, it was pretty early in the morning, and there was little or no other traffic on the highway. Billy became jittery and mouthy after he observed a highway sign that said, "Pont Pierre Laporte."

"What's that mean, 'Pont Laporte'?" he asked.

"It's French, Billy," I replied, "for the Laporte Bridge, which brings you into downtown."

"Pull over, I want to piss on this province!" he shouted in his customary, abrasive way.

"I don't think you want to do that, man," I said. "You'll find that the Quebec cops are not as nice as your OPP or Windsor police. You piss on the side of the roadway here, and they'll kick your ass and ask questions later. I'll stop at the next service station."

"Okay, man," Billy said, a little more timid.

Meanwhile, I wished I could slap him silly. Maybe if I stopped, I could get my colleagues from Quebec City to do it for me. Not a good idea, I reminded myself. I just had to be calm. His day would come.

The trip continued until we arrived in La Pocatiere, where I saw a twenty-four-hour service station and decided to drop in so that Billy and the rest of us could relieve ourselves. I filled the gas tank while my two cohorts went inside.

When I went inside to pay, I observed Billy using the five-finger discount to relieve the service station of a few snacks from the counter.

Damn, Billy, I thought. *Can't you just pay for that stuff from the money we stole from that lady before leaving Windsor?*

I guessed it was just in his blood. He was a crook. I was worried that he, along with my vehicle and me, were on a surveillance camera and that a member of the Surete du Quebec (SQ), the Quebec version of the OPP, would pull us over a few kilometers down the road. The officers would pay close attention to three losers in a car with Ontario plates after receiving a complaint from a tired night clerk at the service station. That's all I needed, to be brought to a police station as a co-conspirator in the theft of a miserable chocolate bar, only to have the operation and my cover blown by a well-meaning night shift patrolman who was excited about having to respond to a real call at that time of night.

"Billy, for Christ's sake, smarten up," I whispered. "I'm about three hours from home, and I don't want to spend a night in jail and miss that court appearance for my kids."

He shook his head and headed out to the car without paying for his chocolate bar. Ah well, it was going be worth watching that bastard get arrested and locked up when we got back to Windsor. In the meantime, I had to remain calm. I was getting tired and impatient, but I could not show it for fear that one of those assholes would offer to drive.

The driving in the Bas-St-Laurent was easy—not much traffic, good roads, and I was getting closer to dropping those guys off. I still wondered where my spin team was. I hadn't seen any of the boys since we had left Windsor fifteen hours earlier. They were either very good or they were lost and I was all alone with my two buddies. I had done a lot of surveillance in my career, and I was optimistic that they were not far away. As I mentioned, there was not much traffic, so it was difficult for them to get too close, but I was confident they were not far away. I remembered a conversation with one of the boys before we left Windsor who said he was stationed at the Bathurst RCMP detachment at one time, so I wasn't concerned that they could not keep up to me.

The trip was becoming difficult for everyone, I was sure. Travelling such a long distance with the traffic of Toronto, Montreal, and then Quebec City was tough enough, and now we were driving on what seemed to be an endless road with no signs of life except for the occasional house off the highway. I was sure the spin team was tired. I certainly was. My two friends were enjoying nice, albeit short, naps, especially when I purposely hit some bumps to keep myself awake and to ensure they were not too comfortable. I kept myself vigilant with thoughts of the job going well and the upcoming reunion with my wife and kids. I couldn't help but reminisce about life and career, family, and the brotherhood of police officers.

This is good, Luc, I told myself. *You're good, handsome, and smart. They're bad, ugly, and not too bright. You're the king of the world.* Then I thought, *Wow, I'm losing it!* I concluded such thoughts were my mind's way of staying focused and awake. I giggled inside and promised myself that once the trip was over, I was due for a visit with my shrink. He would talk me back down to Earth, or so I hoped.

We reached Riviere-du-Loup, which meant we were just an hour away from my beloved New Brunswick. The four-lane highway after Riviere-du-Loup narrowed to two lanes. It became a little easier to stay awake, but it required more concentration, because we kept meeting large tractor trailers of lumber entering Quebec from New Brunswick. The traffic was heavier, because the road was one of only two entries into New Brunswick from the northwest. I couldn't pass vehicles at will, and I had to be careful in the early morning hours so as not to run head-on into an oncoming vehicle or a humungous moose.

Moose are beautiful, majestic animals when they are on the roadside, but they're deadly when standing in the middle of the roadway facing down a car travelling at one hundred kilometres an hour. They have long legs, which help them walk through marshes looking for food and run fast when hunters try to kill them for their great steaks and roasts. However, their long legs on a highway ensure that, when struck by a vehicle, their large body falls onto the oncoming vehicle, crushing the bumper, hood, roof, and everything under it, including people. Such accidents are not a pretty sight. Lives are lost on a regular basis with accidents involving moose and cars. It is also a known fact that moose like to eat grass from the side of the highway, since it is salty from our transport department laying salt on the highways during winter. As a result, I was being extra careful, driving a little slower, but just fast enough to reach the border an hour and a half later and drop my buddies at Ken's sister's place.

My passengers were still sleeping when I entered New Brunswick. I woke them up by welcoming Ken home and welcoming Billy to my home province. They were both rested and seemed content to have finally arrived.

After getting directions from Ken, I headed for the small village on the outskirts of Grand Sault, where his sister lived. I was going to question him about what his sister and brother-in-law did for a living, but it became obvious that they were involved in one way or another with the growing of potatoes. We drove past kilometer after kilometer of potato fields, and I could imagine that everyone was involved in the potato industry in one fashion or another.

That part of northwestern New Brunswick produces potatoes and is home to the world-renowned McCain potato chip company. The potatoes are exported all over the world, and New Brunswick and PEI are the two largest growers and sellers. As in my part of the province, where there are many fishermen, the economy relies on potatoes to ensure the survival of many. When the harvest is weak, people have to leave to find a year-round job.

Ken did not like the life of farmer, harvester, or factory worker, so he left for Windsor, where he had relatives who would help him find a job and make something of himself. However, along with full-time work came more money, and with more money, more fun. Then he did something stupid because of his drug use and lost his job. So, like many others, he turned to crime to survive.

Ken liked illegal drugs, but he couldn't always pay for them, so he sold his own. Why not? Except for the cops, no one bothered him. He was a smart guy, but by hanging out with losers, he had become a loser. I believe that his cooperation with the cops and me might have helped him realize it was time to get on with his life away from the West End gang, who wase causing him a lot of trouble. It was actually a blessing in disguise that the police had offered to pay him for his work and to assist him with a serious offence in front of the courts. Maybe things would work out. Secretly, I wished him well.

At about 0600 hours on March 19, I finally arrived in the yard of Ken's sister's house on the outskirts of Grand Sault. It didn't take long for Ken and Billy to get out, grab their clothes, and walk towards the house. I laid my head back, took a long, deep breath, and thanked the Lord for having taken me that far without any major incident. I also thought about Ken's poor sister. She didn't know Billy. I didn't know her either. Maybe she was a party animal and a drug user like her little brother.

Her place was a typical farmhouse, large with a nice front porch, and it looked well maintained. I conclude that she and her husband were hard-working farmers and that Ken was the wayward child of the family. I wished her luck with those two and then headed back to the highway.

Where was my spin team? I hoped they were not lost and that I didn't have to go looking for them. I was too tired, and I wanted to go home to Bathurst, which was another three hours away. I was relieved to see one of the boys in his vehicle parked in the lot of Daigle's Motel. After finding a more discreet location in the lot, the other team members arrived.

Following greetings and kudos, the team leader told me that he had kept in communication with the Windsor office and that all went well, that Billy's admission had been recorded, and that everything was good so far. I felt an enormous wave of pride and happiness. I was so proud and pleased that the troops had kept up to me and ensured nothing bad would happen. Everyone was in great spirits, tired but satisfied that we had made it that far. The team leader related that the trip had been uneventful except for that part between Kingston and closer to Montreal when I had accelerated to 160 kph. They had tried to catch up but were unsuccessful. They had also taken the agreed-upon Route 20 on the south side of Montreal while I had taken AutoRoute 40, which took me onto the island of Montreal, through the Tunnel Hypolite Lafontaine, and then back onto Route 20, heading for Quebec City. The team felt bad about having lost me in the traffic, and I could just imagine their panic at not being able to locate me. Those things happened. I realized that when Billy was explaining his involvement and subsequent murder of Ronald Lougheed, I was completely focused on his words and lost track of my speed and direction when I took the turn onto the island rather then follow the south shore. I would have to be more careful on the return trip.

I was also worried that Billy and Ken were together away from the gang and away from the cops and that Ken might feel bad and tell Billy what was going on, along with the fact that I was a cop. I would need to assess them carefully once they got into the car. If I had any doubts, I would cancel the return trip. I advised the spin team that we had about another three hours to reach Bathurst, where my buddy, Gary Legresley, had reserved rooms for them.

After our chat, I felt invigorated and knew that we had done the job properly, with the expected results, and that the boys in Windsor, including Brags and Neal, would be jumping for joy. Well, maybe not jumping, but I knew they would be happy, as would the entire team and their superiors. I was pretty confident that Chief Armstrong would be happy and that my lovely wife and our kids would be proud of their old man.

At the same time, I had been on the job for many years, and I knew that if something could go wrong, it would go wrong. Call me pessimistic, but I prefer realistic. Only when Billy was back home in Windsor and in custody would I be able to breathe easier and relax. Then I could go home and carry on with my life. In the meantime, I was looking forward to a long sleep in my own bed and some down time to rejuvenate.

The trip along the north of the province was uneventful at seven in the morning except for a line-up of unmarked police cars cruising at a good speed on our way to the Atlantic Host Hotel in Bathurst, where I had a good breakfast with the team. I left them and went home, only to discover that my wife and girls were out of town for a gymnastics competition. I was disappointed, but in hindsight, it was probably better that they were out. I could write my notes from the trip and then take a long rest.

After completing my notes, I decided to call Neal for an update on what was going on. Neal congratulated me on the good work and wondered if the local police in Grand Sault should arrest Billy and then transfer him back to Ontario. That brought on several scenarios, all of which involved various police forces, crown attorneys, judges, and so on. If arrested in New Brunswick, Billy would be locked up until the New Brunswick courts completed all of the necessary paperwork to release him to Ontario law enforcement. It was wishful thinking on my part that it would happen. Besides, Neal mentioned that it would solidify the court procedures and the case if I could get Billy to tell me where he had hidden or disposed of the gun. Needless to say, a quick decision was made that I would pick up my two friends and return to Windsor as planned, where they would be arrested. Neal hoped that the trip back would give me occasion to be more forceful with Billy in obtaining the location of the weapon. He said he would get back to me about the next step in my adventure.

I also told him that I wanted to inform the Grand Sault Police that they had a couple of criminals in their midst and, should any crimes occur, that Billy and Ken could certainly be considered as suspects. Grand Sault is a small town made up of hard-working Acadian farmers and small business owners located a few kilometers from the American border, and it has a low crime rate. I wanted the police to be aware but not so conspicuous that they awakened any doubts in the minds of my friends. I wanted to let them know that Billy and Ken were around, but I would ask them not to start twenty-four-hour surveillance on them. That would only cause Ken and Billy to panic and do something stupid.

I made the call to Chief Michaud of the Grand Sault police and informed him of the visitors staying just outside his town. I gave him a quick briefing of the operation and added that if there were any problems or strange crimes in his community, the Ontario visitors were more than likely involved. Chief Michaud thanked me for the heads up and added that he would inform the shift commanders but that no special interest would be made for the visitors. I thanked him and then telephoned

Chief Armstrong, my boss, and briefed him on what was going on. He congratulated me and then asked where my car was parked.

"Geez, it's in the driveway, Chief," I stated.

"Get that car away from your home, dummy!" he shouted. "If your friend's Grand Falls buddies come looking and find the wheels in your driveway, it could be dangerous for your wife and kids!"

Okay, boss, I thought. *Thanks for the nice words of encouragement.* I knew he was right, but after being awake for close to twenty-four hours in a stressful situation, my brain wasn't working properly.

"Take the goddam car and park it somewhere in a public place far from your home," he said.

Good idea. I jumped into the car and parked it in the parking lot of a used car garage not far from my place. Then I walked back to my house. It was enough to leave me completely exhausted. I don't even remember hitting the bed, and I slept like a baby for over twelve hours. I had one day to catch up on some sleep and get hyped up for the Saturday morning return trip. It would be a long trip, but I knew the operation would end soon. I had to get the location of that gun. That was all we needed to make the case tight as hell.

On Friday morning, I proceeded to the RCMP Station in Bathurst, where I obtained another battery for my cell phone transmitter and called

Neal. He probably understood from our early conversation that I was exhausted and that it was a long car drive from Bathurst to Windsor. Neal suggested that we drive to Kingston on Saturday, take a room at the Comfort Inn, and stay the night.

"During the evening," he continued, "you should get a case of beer and a pizza and invite Ken and Billy to your room to watch the hockey game or something. Get on the topic of the weapon again, and see if Billy will divulge its location. I've reserved two rooms for you at the Comfort Inn. All you have to do is stop there, walk in, tell them you're Luc Landry, and they'll give you a room, which we will have wired up. Then invite them in, shoot the breeze for a while with a good beer, and later on, get up and tell them you're gonna go pick up a pizza at a pizzeria located near the motel. When you're gone, I'm sure they'll talk about you, and maybe Billy will actually tell Ken where the gun is."

"You never know," I said. "It might work."

I made sure that Neal would brief the RCMP boys or whoever was going to spin me from the Quebec border to Windsor, and I was set to go. I was not too pleased about having to drive back to Windsor, but it had to be done, and hopefully I would be able to get Billy to tell me where the gun was.

I returned home to prepare my regular Friday steak and shrimp supper. With a good bottle of homemade red wine, I figured I would sleep quite well before the long journey back to Ontario.

It was at such times that I missed my family. I was thankful for my strong wife who had stuck with me through thick and thin. She had been a military wife and was used to running the house and caring for our kids while I was away. I wondered sometimes how the hell she did it.

Our life together had begun a long time earlier when we met in high school. She was in the Anglophone part of school while I attended the francophone school, which, in those days, was in the same building. I noticed her for the first time while I was washing dishes in the school cafeteria. She was sitting at a table playing cards with her girlfriends. I was interested in her right away. As the days went by, I noted that she was a cheerleader for our basketball team. Whenever I scored a basket, she would give a cheer for me. I know I'm not that bright, but I concluded that each cheerleader had a player assigned to her and, when he scored, she was responsible for leading a cheer while the others backed her up. Her assignment just happened to be me.

We started talking and playing cards, which she always beat me at, and one thing led to another. I invited her to my family Christmas Eve celebrations, which consisted of midnight mass and then the return to our house for my mom's "Reveillon," a get together with family and friends where we ate homemade meat pies made with rabbit and partridge and her famous chicken bouillon. The older members of my family had a couple of drinks, and Dad played the fiddle while my sisters sang old family favorites. I don't remember ever seeing my father intoxicated or drinking, for that matter, but as my mother said, "He has a couple of shots, takes out the violin, gets his daughters to sing, then he cries, then he goes to bed." It was a wonderful way for my date to meet the clan. It would help her decide whether to stay with me and this crazy bunch or move on to a saner yet boring relationship. Coming from a large family herself, she had probably witnessed something similar in her clan. At any rate, it stuck, and we stayed together as girlfriend/boyfriend.

Following high school, I left to join the military police. After training, I was stationed in Val D'Or, "the Valley of Gold," QC, a nuclear weapons storage site. Then I returned to marry my bride. We settled in a small, one-bedroom apartment in Val D'Or, and she learned the hard way what it was like to be married to a soldier. Life was difficult, but we enjoyed our country, and we enjoyed each other.

Over the years, the kids came along. With my frequent absences for training or operations, Lise stayed behind with them and did a wonderful job of raising them. Therefore, it was not unusual, and

I was not surprised, that she and the girls were out of town at a competition. She was quite involved in her rhythmic gymnastics club, which my two daughters were part of, and it was something that we both understood. I would return to Windsor, finish my job, and then return to my wife and kids. In the meantime, I was home alone with our dog, Scrappy, and the perfect steak and seafood meal, which, as usual, Scrappy shared with me.

After the good meal and wine, I turned the TV off and headed for bed. I hoped I could fall asleep quickly and get a good night's rest. It was going to be a long drive back to Windsor.

As I laid there in bed, many thoughts crossed my mind. What kind of shape would the guys be in? Had Ken told Billy in a moment of guilt that I was a cop? Could I get Billy to tell me where he had hidden the weapon? A dozen questions ran through my head, ruining my wishes for a good night's sleep. There was nothing else I could do to complete the job that we had not thought of already. We had Billy on the admission that he killed Lougheed. That was good enough for me, but it sure would be icing on the cake if I could find that gun. It was just a matter of staying cool and not being too pushy about the evidence.

10

BACK TO WINDSOR

At 0800 hours on Saturday, March 21, I left my residence and proceeded to the Atlantic Host Motel to meet up with my spin team and then head on to Grand Sault. The weather was fine with a blue sky and was warming up, so I informed the team leader that we could go through the Resources Road and save one hour of driving from Bathurst. The Resources Road was known locally as the road that led to all of the local iron ore mines. It connected Bathurst on the east to the town of St. Quentin in the west part of the province. We would save an hour by going straight across rather than following the coast, as we had done on the way in. It was a faster route, but it was also uninhabited with rough terrain, especially in spring. The team leader agreed, and off we went.

My relationship with the RCMP spin team was cordial and professional, but I wondered what they thought of UCs. Did they really care about them or was it just another job? I had seen handlers who did not care for the UC. He was just one tool in a large box of law enforcement techniques and tactics, and the job consisted of attaining that goal, no matter what it was, at any cost. That was not how I thought of my relationship with the spin team, but I had not sat down long enough with any of them to hear their opinion on the job and especially on me. They had been brought in to assist the Windsor police on a Windsor police case, and I was worried they didn't care as much as I thought they should. But I concluded they were top-of-the-line professionals who would ensure my protection at all costs. All I cared was that they remembered that I would be returning to Windsor through Quebec on Highway 20, through the Hypolite Lafontaine Tunnel in Montreal, onto Highway 15 and the Boulevard Metropolitain on the island, and then take the 40 to the border and Highway 401. I had used that highway most of my adult life, and I was confident that I wouldn't get lost even if in a stressful situation with my two buddies.

Once the briefing was complete, all of the cars were gassed up, and each member was equipped with a double/double from Tim Horton's. We left Bathurst with me in the lead until we arrived in St.

Quentin, where the team got into their spin mode and I lost them in the light traffic. An hour later, I was driving into Ken's sister's driveway.

I didn't even have to get out of the vehicle, because Ken and Billy came strolling down the hill from the house and jumped into the car. After quick greetings, I noted the strong smell of stale cigarettes mixed with booze, and I figured they must have been partying all night.

"How was your visit?" I asked.

"It was great," Billy said. "I had the chance to go skiddooing in the back woods. That's something we don't do in Windsor, and I felt like a million dollars."

Ken, on the other hand, did not answer and appeared to be in a bad mood, most likely caused by the stress of having Billy visiting his sister, the drinking, and the lack of sleep. Ken's sister had already served them a nice breakfast, so there was no need to stop for coffee.

As I drove, I tried to figure out a way to let them know that we would be stopping in Kingston overnight. I told them about my meeting with the lawyers and the court and informed them that it did not look too good for me to get custody of the kids. The judge didn't hold back when he said that I was a drunk and a druggie, that I had lost my wife, and that he would certainly not give me access to the kids, especially now that I was living in Ontario. No matter how I tried to explain to him that I had moved to Ontario to straighten up and get off dope so I could return healthier and financially secure and then offer my kids a better life, the judge didn't buy it. He told me that when I came home on holidays, I could call my lawyer, and maybe social services would allow me to have a supervised visit or two.

Billy voiced his opinion on family court judges, which I will not repeat here. It was good to see that Billy had accepted my rendition of the court case as I complained about having made such a long trip for nothing.

"Well, Luc, you had to try, man," he said.

"Yeah, well, at least I got to talk to the old lady, and I think we're going to attempt to get together again once I get myself together. She even gave a me a hundred bucks for the trip back."

Ken offered no comment. He seemed to be trying to get some shut eye. I obliged, and so did Billy as we drove on the Trans-Canada to the Belle Province.

As I said earlier, if something could go bad, it would. We hadn't been on the highway long when, once again, my heavy foot drew the attention of a patrol officer who was on the roadside with his radar pointed directly at me. Didn't those guys have anything better to do?

The officer jumped out of his car and pointed me over to the side. I obliged and, now that we had Billy's admission, I figured, wwhat the hell, maybe he'd arrest us and we'd spend the night in a warm, comfy jail cell until the leader of the spin team vouched for me and I was released. Not so lucky!

The officer addressed me politely in broken English. When I answered in French, he reverted to his mother tongue and told me I was going 129 kph in a 100 zone and that he was going to give me a ticket.

I handed him my papers, and he returned to his vehicle. Ten minutes later, he returned and told me to watch my speed and to have a nice day. There was no complaining from Billy or Ken, especially since I had told Billy earlier that it wasn't wise to give Quebec cops a hard time.

Another fine. I knew Neal might be able to call his counterpart in Ontario, but I didn't think he could do the same thing in Quebec. Later, I called the office where the officer was stationed and informed them of the situation. They told me not to worry, that the summons would be cancelled. Good guys. It occurred to me that if I had not done that, my cover name would still be on file. If I ever travelled through Quebec again while undercover, I would have had to have my actual papers or else I would be held for unpaid fines.

After receiving the ticket, I returned to the highway and headed toward Ontario. The trip was uneventful after that except for the weather which, as usual, started getting lousy around Riviere-du-Loup. Light snow continued until past Rimouski, where the highway followed the Fleuve Saint-Laurent, and the winds were fierce and gusty. The traffic was light, being a Saturday, and I figured we would make good time to Montreal. At that time, I would have to be creative and figure out a way to tell the boys that we would be staying overnight in Kingston.

That turned out to be pretty easy, because, on our approach to Montreal, I could not see ten feet in front of me due to the steady spring snow and the other vehicles spraying my windshield as we drove bumper to bumper at about forty kph.

"Shit, Luc, you can't see where you're going," Billy remarked.

"Yeah, it's tough," I replied, "but it should be okay when we get out of this traffic on the other side of the island."

But it wasn't.

"I hope you guys got a few bucks left," I said. "I think we'll pull over for the night around Kingston."

"Yeah, yeah," was the response.

I smiled to myself and thanked the Big Guy for his wisdom, guidance, and especially his snowfall.

Finally, we got out of Montreal and headed west on Highway 40 to catch the 401 when entering Ontario. Where was my spin team? Had I lost them again?

As I was thinking that, one of the boys flew by me at a high rate of speed, and I deduced that the team leader wanted me to see someone, thus ensuring my comfort and peace of mind. That they did. I'm not sure if it was the RCMP spin team or the Windsor boys who were supposed to pick me up at the border. I assumed it was a member of the Windsor team letting me know I was their baby now. It felt good to be back with them. I remember some of the boys being upset when Neal told them they had no authority outside of Ontario and that they were not able to stay with me until we reached NB, so it was nice to see them again. I understood that the RCMP spin team was also on their way to Windsor, so I felt special when I thought of two teams of four vehicles tailing me. It was nice to be loved!

The change from the 40 to the 401 did not affect the weather in any way. In fact, it seemed to get worse with a lot more traffic. I continued in the storm and did my best to maintain control of the vehicle.

As I drove, I told Billy that when I was home, I had reflected on him telling me that he had shot Lougheed. "What did you do with the gun, Billy?" I asked. "You know that's probably what's going to put the last nail in the coffin if the cops are able to find it."

"Don't worry about that, man," he said. "There are only two people who know where that gun is. That's me and the dead guy, and nobody else will ever know."

It appeared funny to me the way he answered, and for a second I wondered if he had buried the weapon with Lougheed. I had to make sure that Neal and the boys knew that. I wasn't sure if the communications were still working in the bad weather, and I told myself that I better not forget to tell them about Billy's declaration.

Other than that bit of conversation, we didn't talk about anything else. Ken and Billy drifted in and out of sleep and, again, Ken was very quiet. It became clear to me that he had had enough of the story. He wanted to get home soon so they could arrest Billy and get him out of his life. The feeling was mutual, and I knew he had a lot more to lose than me, so I did not ask him to put any more pressure on Billy.

After one of their short snoozes, they started a short conversation about some guy they called "Gilles." I wasn't sure where they had met him, either Windsor or Grand Sault, but they didn't like him. I figured he was someone they had met in Grand Sault. Ken said that he had had a bad dream about him.

"I had a knife to that fucker's throat," Billy said. "I don't like that guy, and he's lucky to be alive."

I dreaded the thought of my Grand Sault colleagues responding to a fight in a bar and finding a male subject with his throat slit and no suspects to be found, because they were now on their way back to Ontario with me. But it turned out my worries were for nothing.

"It's a good thing for him that we got out of there when we did," Billy said.

We continued through the storm until we reached the sign for Kingston. I told the boys that was it, we were going to take a motel for the night. I saw the sign for the Day's Inn and made my way slowly to the front door. Neal had informed me that rooms 103 and 107 were reserved in my name. All I had to do was walk up to the front desk and the clerk would hand me the key. Billy said he would accompany me, because he had to use the washroom.

When I reached the front desk, Billy continued on to the washroom. I wasn't sure if the clerk knew what was up, and that was confirmed after I gave him my name.

"Sorry, sir," he said, "I don't have a reservation for you."

Oh now! Someone had screwed up. Why would Neal tell me he had reserved the rooms if that was not the case?

After a moment of panic, an unknown male approached me. "You got the wrong motel, man," he whispered. "You have reservations at the Comfort Inn across the road."

Shit. A few seconds later, Billy returned from the washroom. I had just enough time to turn and walk towards the door when he asked what was up.

"There's no more room here," I said. "The clerk told me there might be rooms across the street at the Comfort Inn." I mumbled something about how I sure as hell hoped there were rooms there, because it was getting too dangerous to continue on the highway.

Billy agreed, and we jumped in the car and proceeded to the Comfort Inn. I observed a beer store and a pizza joint nearby. God bless Neal. I was impressed again by that gentleman's skills.

I went up to the front desk, got the room keys, and returned to the vehicle, where my friends were waiting. I gave Ken a key to room 107. I kept the key to room 103 and told them that they could pay me back when we got to Windsor.

I took my luggage to the room and then returned and informed them that I was going to the nearby beer store and pizza joint. Half an hour later, I returned to my room and, via telephone, invited them over for pizza and beer. Neal had informed me earlier that both rooms were wired and that anything we said would be recorded.

As we feasted on beer and pizza, we discussed everything from the weather to hockey and our family problems. I steered the conversation back to the murder and told Billy that he should absolutely be sure of where he hid the gun.

"That's the one thing that will hang you," I said.

"I know," he replied. "No one knows, and no one will ever know what I did with that gun. Only Lougheed and I know where it is."

I concluded that Billy had hidden the murder weapon and that we would never know what he did with it. But the fact he told me that he had hidden the weapon was enough for a reasonable person to believe he had hidden it for a reason, the reason being that, if it had not been discharged into Lougheed's head, there was no need to hide it. I concluded that, although finding the gun was important, his statement was good enough. It would have been nice to have solid evidence of the weapon, fingerprints, blood, DNA, and so on, but I kept telling myself that we could proceed without it and still get a guilty verdict.

I initiated no further talk on the subject but hoped our conversation would return to it. It was not to be. Billy was slightly interested in the hockey game on TV, Ken looked tired and bored, and so was I. We sat there for another hour, drank some beers and ate pizza, and then they decided to hit the sack.

I sat in the room and thought about Billy's admission and all the comments he had made during the trip so far and hoped that the Windsor boys were as confident as I was that the case was solid. I was not a prosecutor and certainly not a defense lawyer, so whatever legal jargon and tactics they would use was out of my control. I could not dwell on the negative. I had been a cop for many years, and I knew when someone was guilty of a crime. I trusted my instincts and was going to bed confident that Billy had done it, so I would let the other professionals deal with him. That night, I slept like a baby.

At 0930 hours on March 22, we left the motel and got back on the road for the final leg of the trip. Once again, the boys were quiet, and there was not much conversation until we stopped in Cambridge for lunch. I observed Ken handing Billy what appeared to be cash. Billy must have blown his share of the Windsor purse scam and was bumming money from his buddy to pay for lunch. What a man, what a life. Such a waste of a person. Billy would be returning to Windsor having learned nothing about the good life. When arrested, it would probably be just another event in his loser life.

In my more reflective moments, I wondered how a person in Canada could be so lost and uncaring yet portray himself as a proper person. Was it the dope? His upbringing? It certainly was not his health. He appeared to be a strong, healthy individual who simply had to sit down, ponder his life, and try to make it better. It was probably too late. Upon our arrival in Windsor, he would be arrested, locked up, go to trial, be found guilty, and then go to the penitentiary, where he would continue his criminal life, living with his peers in a closed and dangerous environment. I was so glad my father had disciplined me when I was a kid. Otherwise I could have turned out like Billy.

As we approached Windsor, the conversation stopped, and I had a strange feeling. Both men were extremely quiet, and I could almost feel the air of depression setting in. I, on the other hand, felt like a million bucks. This was it, finally. These guys would be out of my hair and out of my life forever. I thought about our stop at the Cambridge restaurant when Ken had handed the cash to Billy. Why hadn't Billy asked me for money? There was no doubt in my mind that he still did not trust me completely as a friend, which was fine by me. Or maybe he was starting to reconnect with his Windsor life, with the murder he had committed, and returning to his dreary way of life. Maybe he regretted going to New Brunswick with me and admitting that he had killed Lougheed. Whatever was going on, they were both very quiet and probably resigned to returning to their miserable way of life.

Well, my friend, I thought, *your life will not be boring for the next few years.* Once we arrived in Windsor, the police welcome wagon would ensure that there was enough excitement to keep Billy entertained for a long while.

When we arrived in Windsor, I felt satisfied. First, I had made it back in one piece. Second, I believed I had done a good job and that justice would be served for the Lougheed family and Ron Lougheed's friends. That was a pretty good feeling. I also thought of my brother and sister officers in Bathurst and Windsor and hoped I had made them proud.

I dropped Billy at his place on Wellington and then drove Ken back to his place. He had done a great job, and I thanked him for it. He was still silent. We shook hands, and I told him that I would see him later when I returned for the trial.

It had been another nineteen hour trip, but for some reason, it had seemed a lot faster than the trip to New Brunswick. I concluded it was simply knowing I had done what was asked of me, with the exception of getting Billy to divulge the location of the murder weapon. All in all though, it was a job well done. Now it was time to let the legal machine begin its work.

After leaving Ken's place, a spin team member approached and told me to follow him. We proceeded to the safe house, where all the boys were in attendance: the Windsor detectives, technicians, the RCMP spin team, and the Windsor spin team. During the briefing, they informed me that Billy was under surveillance and would probably be arrested in the morning. I was happy and enjoyed the moment. We had a good meal, a few drinks, and told war stories until a bunch of exhausted cops went to their homes and families. Lucky guys! Soon, I would be on my way to my family as well.

As promised, Billy was arrested in downtown Windsor early the next morning and taken to the station. I attended the building and, after accepting kudos from all of the other service members, made my way down to the cell block area, where Billy was being held and would be interrogated by Perp and Cliff.

Billy was sitting in an interview room looking a bit cocky. He had his ball cap on but was not as mouthy as I knew he could be. I guessed that was the feeling a person got when his life flashed before his eyes and he was uncertain about his future. Cliff and Perp informed me that they had read him his rights and that he wanted a lawyer. He had called a lawyer but got no answer, so he left a message. Meanwhile, the boys did not interview him.

I informed Perp and Cliff that, after completing my previous undercover operations, I had introduced myself to the suspect as a cop and not the person he or she thought I was. I asked them if it was okay to enter the room to talk to Billy and reveal my true identity. I really liked the look on the suspects' faces when I told them I was a cop. Some smiled, some reacted in anger, and some even said, "I knew it. I knew there was something wrong with you." Well, dummy, if you knew I was a cop, why did you admit to your crime?

Billy was a bit different. When I entered the room, he had a look of surprise on his face.

"What are you doing here, man?" he asked.

"How you doing, Billy?" I said. "I'm not who you think I am. My name is Josh Ouellette, and I'm a police officer from Bathurst, New Brunswick."

Billy's face turned red, and a look of despair appeared in his eyes. There was a short pause, and then he pulled himself up in his chair, straightened his ball cap, and looked me in the eye. "I'll do my twenty-five, man, I'll do my twenty-five."

By that point, I had done close to one hundred undercover jobs, and each time, I noted that look of despair in the suspect's eyes. They were caught. They had told an undercover policeman that they had committed a crime, and now they were totally depressed and thinking, "What the hell do I do now? What's going to happen to me?" It was the reaction for which I had been looking.

"Good luck. See you later, man," I said. Then I left the room, thanked the boys, left the building, and prepared for my plane trip back to my little heaven in Bathurst.

Shortly afterwards, Wahoo and Rainone were also arrested and charged with obstruction of justice for dumping the body and disposing of the vehicle that was used to haul the body to the dump site.

11
HOME AGAIN

I had returned home to my regular police job. The routine was getting to me, and I looked forward to hearing from Neal about the preparations for the trial and for the date to be set. Finally, I was told to report to Windsor in January for testimony in the second-degree murder trial against Billy. The trial would be with judge and jury and would last for a couple of weeks. I had no idea how long I would be there but figured it would only be for my time on the stand. But, as I have said many times, if something can go wrong, it will go wrong, and that time was no different.

In December 1998, I scheduled my annual doctor's visit, as required by our department. I was a bit tired, but I was always tired, so what the hell. After the checkup, I asked the doctor if he could put me on rest for a week. My son was coming to visit from university, and I wanted to spend time with the family. The doctor looked at me with a weird smile and said, "No problem," then filled out a prescription paper. He handed the paper to me, and when I looked at it, my blood pressure went through the roof.

"I just need a week, doc, not three months."

"Listen to me, Mr. Ouellette, you are a police officer, so I'm sure you've seen injured people in a traffic accident?"

"Yeah, so?"

"The difference between the injuries received by the ones you've seen is that you might not have physical cuts and bruises, but you're still hurting. It's more like you've been hit by a bus and your injuries are all in your head. You're burned out, young fellow. Take some time off. I'm sure you'll feel much better after a long rest."

Shit, what was I supposed to do? Billy's trial was in January, and the doctor had just put me on sick leave until March. I had to call Neal to let him know as soon as possible.

After two hours of biting my nails and feeling worried sick about letting the boys down, I called Neal. Although disappointed, he agreed that I should take some time off. He would contact the crown to see about changing the trial date.

As I waited, thousands of questions raced through my mind. Would they change the date? Would they drop the charges? I also worried about all of the good people I would be letting down due to a sickness I didn't even know I had. The worries ruined my day, and rather than being happy that I would be able to spend some time with my family, I was angry that I wasn't able to do my job.

When Neal finally called, he said the crown was not happy, but they would ask the judge to postpone the trial until late spring. I was thankful and finally felt comfortable enough to start the long process of healing my mind as the doctor wished. It was something I was not used to and something I didn't like. I knew my brother and sister officers would talk—Is he really nuts or is he faking it? Most officers suffered in their heads more than I did but would not admit it. At the time, it was rare for an officer to face his demons rather than kicking them out of the way and continuing with life.

In hindsight, it was probably the best time for me to be off. My career had had many highs and lows, and I had accepted that the job was not for the weak. Even if an officer felt weak, he or she was not allowed to display any sign of weakness to anyone, including his or her peers. I had heard the old army saying, "Suck it up, buddy," all my life, so it was a bit strange for me to accept the fact that I could be suffering burnout. Although a bit embarrassed that I had a weakness, I was sure many people had noted that I had several other weaknesses. I would have to accept it and learn to live with it. Geez, and I thought I was Superman. Life is good!

Due to my forced rest, Billy's trial was postponed to a later date while Ross and Rainone had their trial dates set for February 1998. Rainone, who had been charged for trying to get rid of the car used to haul Lougheed's body to the dump site, was found guilty and sentenced. He refused to testify against Wahoo, saying he had never heard him say he was involved with the murder. He figured the car had been used for something illegal but he did not know what and did not ask. I never met Rainone during my time with Billy, and that confirmed my belief that both Wahoo and Rainone no longer wanted to be around Billy for fear of being charged with the killing. I guess there is some kind of loyalty between crooks, because both he and Billy refused to testify against their buddy. At least Rainone had enough brains to take the stand and tell the court he did not know anything. My friend Billy, on the other hand, was not that bright. Loyal yes, but smart, no.

During Wahoo's trial, the crown attorney called Billy to the stand. Billy stood up and addressed the court, saying he had no intention of testifying. The judge directed Billy to stand in the witness box so that his declaration could be written into the court record.

Billy took the stand, folded his arms to his chest, and refused the court clerk when he asked if Billy preferred the Bible for his oath. "I refuse to testify, your Honor."

"You're refusing to take the oath?" the judge asked. "You won't be sworn in?"

Billy asked the judge if he could speak with his lawyer. Following a short conversation, he returned to the stand. "I've got nothing to say," he said, refusing to take the oath.

The judge had the court officers remove Billy and said he would be cited for contempt of court. That brought the trial to an unforeseen halt and caused it to be postponed until the following week.

With Billy refusing to testify against Wahoo, that left Ken's testimony. The defense had done a good job of describing Ken to the jury as a double crosser, worried only about himself. Ken had a long criminal record and had negotiated an agreement with the police to work with the cops to convict Wahoo and Billy for the murder. The defense was able to show him as a user who could not be trusted by anyone, including the jury, the court, the police, or anyone else. The crown's evidence relied heavily on Ken's testimony, since Billy had refused to implicate his buddy and testify. In the end, Wahoo was acquitted of the charge of obstructing justice in the killing of Ronald Lougheed, and on February 25, 1999, he walked out of court a free man. The fact the jury did not believe Ken, the crown's main witness, was a concern for the crown and the police, because they assumed the same argument would be used in the trial against Billy. That meant the fate of the entire police investigation could come down to my testimony.

So far we were one for two: Rainone was found guilty and Wahoo was acquitted. Billy's trial would certainly be interesting.

12
THE PROCEEDINGS AGAINST BILLY

As a result of my enforced time off, the crown attorney had postponed Billy's preliminary hearing to late November. On the morning of November 30, 1998, Crown Prosecutor Bernardon called me to the stand. After swearing the oath, I faced the jury, who appeared to be interested. I prepared myself for a long and arduous task. They had heard previous testimony from several investigators, the coroner, and other witnesses, but I had no idea what anyone of them had said. I reviewed my notes and tried to refresh my memory as best I could. I could foresee the crown attorney talking to me in a calm manner and asking the question without the "Is it possible, sir?" questions I expected from the defense.

In all my years as a police officer, I had testified hundreds of times on homicides, domestic violence cases, and assaults causing bodily harm, and I was confident I would do well, simply because I always told the truth to the best of my memory. I did not lie or stretch the truth just to get the bad guy. I knew that he or she was guilty, and that simply by telling the truth the jury would reach that conclusion. If not, after close to thirty-five years in law enforcement, I had no other choice but to accept their decision. That was the law! If the police screwed up the investigation somehow and the accused was acquitted, then I feel like hell. But in this case, the Windsor police, in my book, had gone above and beyond to cross their Ts' and dot their I's in this investigation, and my testimony would simply compliment all their hard work, leading to Billy's conviction. That was the kind of pressure I felt on the stand. I knew my testimony would be crucial in the outcome of the trial. I was a police officer. I had nothing to lose or gain if Billy was acquitted or found guilty, but it sure as hell would bother me if he was acquitted because of something I had done wrong or forgotten to do.

I also thought of the victim's family and friends. The whole world would get to know the gruesome details of their son's, brother's, and friend's death. I had to block them out of my mind and concentrate on the questions asked by the crown and the defense. I did not know Lougheed's family or friends. I'm sure they were in the courtroom, but all I knew was that I had to be clear, concise, and tell the story as best I could without embellishment or exaggeration. That was my duty.

After taking the stand, I raised my right arm and swore that I would tell the truth and nothing but the truth, so help me God. Then the crown attorney, Mr. Bernardon, asked me to identify myself and started with questions about my involvement in the case. His questions were straightforward and direct, and I had no trouble explaining the operation to the court. I explained how the Windsor police had asked me to infiltrate a group of criminals in the west end of Windsor, whereby two main targets, Wayne (Wahoo) Ross and William Murdoch McKenzie, were suspected of killing Ronald Lougheed of Windsor by shooting him in the head and then disposing of his body in a local park. I had been introduced to the group by Kenneth Legace, an agent for the Windsor Police and a member of the gang in which McKenzie and Ross were also members. His vehicle had been used to dump the body and then brought to a junkyard for disposal. The worker at the salvage yard saw what appeared to be blood in and on the vehicle and notified police. Subsequently Legace, McKenzie, and Ross became suspects in the crime.

Eventually, Legace turned on his friends and signed an agreement with the police to work as an agent, thus leaving McKenzie and Ross as my targets to approach in an attempt to get an admission to the crime. Originally, the police believed that Ross had committed the murder, but further investigation, including a long trip by car to New Brunswick, produced an admission from Billy that he had done the killing. Not only had I witnessed the admission, it had been documented by recording equipment in the undercover vehicle and convinced the police that Billy was the shooter. I explained the main details of the trip and was able to clarify certain points that the crown wanted the jury to hear.

Mr. Goulan, defense attorney, looked for much more detail. He portrayed me to the jury as a tough biker that his client wanted to impress by telling me that he, not Wahoo, had killed Lougheed.

My testimony continued for several days and, in my mind, was going well. Goulan's tactics of trying to show the jury that I was a big, bad tough guy and that Billy was intimidated and only tried to impress me bothered me, since I felt that, during the time I was in Billy's company, there was no indication that he was afraid of me. Needless to say, it concerned me that the defense might convince the jury that Billy was just a poor, scared, little boy who was bullied by the big, bad, toothless down homer.

After several days of testimony, the judge thanked me and excused me from the witness stand. As I left the courthouse, I wondered what the outcome of the trial would be.

It is common practice, and rightfully so, that witnesses are not permitted to stay in the courtroom while others are testifying so as not to tarnish their evidence. Therefore, I was not aware of any testimony from the detectives, Ken, or any other witnesses who had testified before me, and that did not make it any easier on my nerves. I hoped the jury got it right and brought a bit of justice to the Lougheed family and, in turn, a lot of satisfaction to the police for a job well done.

My testimony and my work done, I took the next flight home to New Brunswick and waited impatiently for the jury's decision.

On Wednesday, June 9, 1999, the judge gave the jury their instructions and then sent them off to deliberate on Billy's fate. It did not take long. They returned with a verdict of guilty, and Billy was taken to the cells to await the judge's decision regarding his sentence.

On Saturday, June 12, 1999 in a special edition, reporter Ellen Van Wageningen of the *Windsor Star* wrote that the presiding judge, His Honor John Brockenshire, had sentenced William Murdock McKenzie to a life sentence with possibility of parole after twelve years. The article also stated that the judge recommended that members of the parole board listen to the wiretaps presented in the trial before they agreed to his early release.

Wow, what a relief! I felt like a million dollars. The fear, the anxiety, the anger, and the sleepless nights of worry had finally come to an end. I had made everyone involved happy—the cops, the crown, my family, my co-workers in New Brunswick, and especially, I hoped, the parents and family of Ron Lougheed. I had never met him, but I felt melancholy every time I thought of him and the family he left behind, who probably loved him very much. He might have been a criminal and a drug user, but he did not deserve to be killed that way. No one deserved that!

In the hours, days, and months that passed, I thought often about my job, my brother and sister officers in Windsor, our justice system, and the drug problem in my country. I spent a lot of time wondering about Lougheed's family. He had been someone's son, brother, boyfriend. How were they feeling?

At the end of July 1999, I received my answer in the form of an envelope from the office of the Windsor police chief. In the envelope was a handwritten letter penned on July 27, 1999 from Ronald Lougheed's family. They had sent it to the police chief's office and asked that it be forwarded to me. That letter will stay in my mind forever. It is the greatest tribute a police officer can ever get. I have cried many tears since receiving it!

Dear Detective Ouellette,

It's time now to write this letter to you from my family.

You touched our lives even though we've never met. How do we express our gratitude to you, except for you to know, we thank you from the bottom of our hearts for all that you did for my brother and us, in helping us to let the grief finally pass, and to let my brother rest in peace?

Too many times it seems that no one cares, and life can be very unfair, but God sent us an Angel and that was you.

We were sorry to read that in your line of work, you never met one nice person. I wish we could have met, I know you would like our family, my brother included. He wasn't a bad person really, he was struggling to survive in a harsh world and his heart was too trusting and good to be in the world he was in. I guess God figured my brother had had enough too, and took him to rest.

You changed me too, because I really thought I should consider another profession. I became tired of caring, tired of giving and I thought that if I could protect my heart, then I could survive.

Now I realized that I was meant to care, I was meant to give, and that I should never let anyone take that from me, because then I would be like them. They are going to pay for their actions.

You've helped a lot of people in your profession and we thank you for that, because we've been on the receiving end and know the relief of knowing what happened to your loved one and for the person or persons.

You never know, maybe someday someone in my family will be an angel for someone else. Maybe through this, we have all learned something.

We thank you for taking a stand when no one else would or could, for not letting fear guide you and for doing what you knew in your heart was right.

May God Bless you and your family and keep you all safe from harm.

Sincerely, The Family of
Ron Lougheed.

As I mentioned earlier, I had completed close to one hundred undercover operations, but I had never received any show of gratitude. I guess I'm wrong to say I never met a nice person in my line of work. The letter from the Lougheed family restored my faith in humanity. I want to use this book to thank them, because I have never met them and probably never will, but, as they say, God works in mysterious ways.

I would like to end this part of the story with the closing words of Ellen Van Wageningen's *Windsor Star* article: "That afternoon, William Murdoch McKenzie, now a convicted murder, was taken back to the Windsor jail. Ouellette, a former undercover officer arrived home and started cutting his lawn."

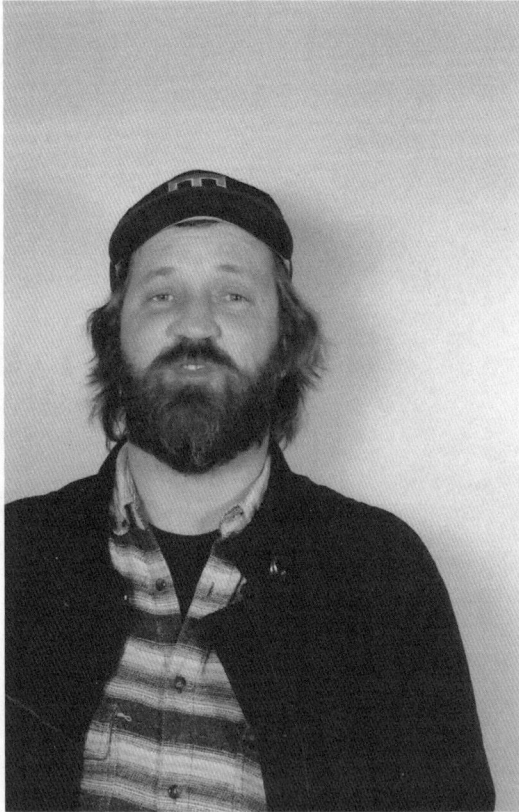

The author in undercover dress.

ABOUT THE AUTHOR

Chief Josh Ouellette CD (retired) is a military police veteran who also served as a municipal police officer in Canada for over forty years. Josh started his law enforcement career at nineteen in the Canadian Forces Military Police. After leaving the military, he went on to serve in several provincial and municipal police forces in New Brunswick before retiring from his law enforcement career, in 2015, as the chief of the BNPP Regional Police Force in northern New Brunswick.

Married for over forty years, Josh and his wife have three adult children and four beautiful grandchildren. They reside in a small fishing village on the northeastern coast of New Brunswick. Josh plans to make The Catching of a Killer the first of many books detailing the over 100 undercover cases with which he was involved throughout New Brunswick, Ontario, and Maine.

Printed in Canada